# Peter Gorton

## AN INVITATION TO COOK

HALSGROVE

First published in Great Britain in 2013

British Library Cataloguing-in-Publication Data
A CIP record for this title is available from the British Library

ISBN 978 0 85704 210 1

**HALSGROVE**

Halsgrove House,
Ryelands Business Park, Bagley Road,
Wellington, Somerset TA21 9PZ
Tel: 01823 653777   Fax: 01823 216796
email: sales@halsgrove.com

Part of the Halsgrove group of companies
Information on all Halsgrove titles is
available at: www.halsgrove.com

Printed in China by Everbest Printing Co Ltd

# Contents

*This book is affectionately dedicated to my*

*wife Kaz, and children Rheanna &, Zac and Sky*

*the dog for their love, patience and support and*

*also to the memory of my late mother.*

# Acknowledgements

I WOULD LIKE TO THANK all the chefs I have worked with and everybody who has helped to make this book happen.

My special thanks go to Margaret Jones for her untiring input and typing skills and also her encouragement, without her I do not think this book would have been possible.

Thanks also to all those companies who have helped in the production of this book. These include Villeroy and Boch, Robert Welch, Howells the Butcher, Country Cheeses, Tamar Valley Fruiterers, and fishmongers S&J Fisheries Ltd, Mathew Stevens & Son and of course Halsgrove Publishing.

Finally I would like to thank my team at Gorton's and especially my Sous chef Alex Parsons for his hard work over the last two years.

# Foreword

I HAVE TRULY enjoyed putting this book together. The book illustrates the food that I cook and serve. It shows respect for quality ingredients and highlights the different types of cuisine I enjoy.

I love eating good food – to me it is one of the great pleasures of life, whether it is an informal meal cooked at home with family and friends, or a culinary feast served in one of the finest restaurants in the world.

Through my years of cooking as a professional chef I have tried to marry natural ingredients one with another to find simple harmonies that enhance rather than overpower. A recipe in my eyes is not to be followed exactly. Try adding the zest of this, drop of that, or maybe a tiny pinch of spice.

Let yourself be led by your palate and heart. I have always cooked to give pleasure and joy and to try to bring closeness between the people I cook for and myself.

Cooking is a matter of interpretation, adaptability and creativity. I have collected many recipes over the years and have added my own personal international touch to this book. I have tried my best to make the recipes accessible to all cooks, and have attempted to limit the amount of hard-to-find ingredients to a minimum.

I have had a wonderful time testing recipes with my chefs and would like to encourage you to have fun with this book. Don't forget to mix and match recipes. Nothing replaces a 'hands on' approach to cooking. The only way to improve is to experiment and make mistakes, so have a go and don't lose heart.

The strongest memories when you visit someone's house are usually the first impression as you arrive and your last impression as you leave. The same can be true of a meal, and because the starter or appetiser is the first course in a meal, it is essential that it should always create a good impression, as should the dessert as it is the last memory.

Bon appétit

*Peter Gorton*

The courtyard at Gorton's.

# Introduction

PAINTERS WOULD MAKE great cooks. The eye for tone and texture, choosing colours that work together, avoiding those that do not; subtle variations revealed only with a closer look, vibrant pigments skilfully transferred from palette to canvas, detail created at the stroke of a brush, the whole combining into a masterpiece, just as the artist intended. Watching Masterchef Peter Gorton at work in his kitchen is to see the artist intent upon his latest creation and, as with the experienced painter, he is completely at one with the practical skills of cookery. But beyond that lies a true artist's temperament, a desire to create a memorable landscape of taste, his signature on each dish as clear as that of Rembrandt or Picasso. In this book Peter's love of food and cooking shines through on every page as does his enthusiasm and his desire to show others how to cook well, and most of all how to enjoy it.

To appreciate the artist it is valuable to know a little about the man.

He was born in 1965 and grew up in the Mumbles area of South Wales, his passion centred on sport especially rugby and he played at a good level for many years. Peter's great Grandfather played for West Glamorgan, his son Zac now shares Peter's passion and love for the game.

His mother's family were from Cardiff, in South Wales. Peter recalls a small woman with a loving but determined character, standing up to anyone who posed a threat to her children. She was also a medium, a trait Peter feels he has inherited and there is no denying a clarity of decision-making in Peter that has allowed him to chart a sure course through life. Tragically his mother died from breast cancer when Peter was just eight years old (he now supports charities devoted to this issue).

Originally from Hartlepool, Peter's Father after leaving the army began a career owning and running laundrettes and he was also a professional singer touring working men's clubs and seaside towns with the young Peter and his sister, Linda, trailing in his wake.

Back home in South Wales, now aged fifteen, Peter earned a little pocket money working in a cafe called 'Sizzles'; 'More like a microwave shop,' Peter laughs, 'a hard place where they danced on the tables on a Saturday night!' What an introduction to catering for Peter.

With Peter now sixteen and his father remarried with a 'new' family of two children to care for, Peter decided it was time to leave home for good. 'I just walked out with my suitcases. There were no real goodbyes.'

Alone and with no money Peter relied upon friends for accommodation. 'Their kind mothers sort of adopted me as an extra family member.' He then met Colin Pressdee who owned the then famous restaurant the Drangway in Swansea, 'a meeting that changed my life,' Peter recalls. 'The chef there was Bryan Webb and they were very much into fine dining. I had never seen food like this and I simply fell in love with it. I learnt a great deal about seafood: turbot and bass would be delivered by the stone; crabs and lobster straight from the Gower coast; oysters were kept in special tanks at the back of the kitchen; and laverbread freshly picked.' There were some early disasters: 'Bryan left me with a sinkful of fish which I convinced him I could clean and fillet. In fact I ruined them all and Brian had to take over. In the long run it was a useful lesson. I learned to listen and to watch experts at work in the kitchen. You are never too old to learn.' With these experiences and under a day-release scheme Peter began to hone the skills that eventual brought him Masterchef status.

At eighteen and now seeking new opportunities Peter left to work at the internationally famous Walnut Tree Restaurant near Abergavenny, then owned by chef Franco Taruschio and his wife Ann. Here, in the kitchen of 'one of the Best Restaurant in Britain' Peter learned the importance of speed in creating fine dishes prepared for a busy restaurant visited by some of the world's greatest cooks and celebrities. 'Elizabeth David was a regular diner.'

'Franco was very innovative; he was one of the first chefs to introduce truffles into British cuisine. His kitchen was spotless but always hectic and full of Italian women, all chewing garlic. Here I learned that hard work was not enough to create great food. Teamwork in a happy environment allowed everything to come together and turned good food into truly great food.'

His three years at the Walnut Tree were among the best experiences of his life, 'but you have to move on as a chef,' and Peter's next move was to Bath, working as third chef at The Priory restaurant under a great chef Michael Collom. For almost two years Peter enjoyed working in the old Roman town but brighter city lights were calling and he moved to London, to Hilaire in Old Brompton Road, under head chef Simon Hopkinson, now best known as a food writer. 'Lots of chefs look back at Simon and recognise that that's where they got their inspiration from. He was a truly inspirational figure to many young chefs like me during the 1980s.' Eventually Hopkinson moved on to Bibendum one of the Capital's most enduring restaurants while Hilaire was taken over by Peter's old mentor, Bryan Webb.

Peter's time as a young chef in the city echoes the experiences of many who have shared this life. 'London is a great place but it can be very lonely too. Living in North Ealing and then Hackney is hardly the most glamorous lifestyle and the brutal hours of restaurant working reduce the opportunities for socialising. Many people see me as confident, even cocky, but I am fundamentally a shy person and I had to make a particular effort to make friends, taking advantage of all that London had to offer, visiting galleries and museums, experiencing the glam side as well as the less glam side of life.'

Now aged 21 Peter decided it was time to travel; to discover more about the food of other cultures. Recognising that Britain was fast becoming a centre of international cuisine he wanted to sample cooking and ingredients in their natural habitat. Using his savings he set off first for Thailand, sampling the best food on offer, then on to Australia. Here he secured a position as sous chef in the prestigious Burnham Beeches Hotel, 40 miles north of Melbourne. This superb Art Deco mansion, converted to a hotel in the 1980s, stands amidst lush gardens; a wildlife paradise. 'You could call down Kookaburras out of the trees and they'd take a piece of meat from your hand, slapping it on your arm as they would have killed their prey before eating it.'

'There's no doubt about it, travelling opened my eyes to the rest of the world and helped me understand in more detail how food and culture are intermixed, how what we eat is truly what we are. Each country has something new to offer the enquiring chef; there's always something new to learn.' Peter smiles and repeats what might well be regarded as his chef's mantra: 'You are only as good as your last meal.'

Japan beckoned next, the six months spent at Burnham Beeches providing the funds to continue his exploration of world food. Peter's time in Australia and the Far East not only provided an education in food, it also taught him other important lessons. 'I suppose I had been lucky up to now in working with so many great chefs who were willing to teach me their skills. They were kind people. Nice people. But I learned that not all those in the industry were so pleasant; petty jealousy, overblown egos and bitterness are also part and parcel of the catering trade and I realised that I needed to toughen up, especially if I were to become a boss in my own right. Learning man-management was just as important as learning cookery skills.

Back home Peter worked in some of the country's best provincial restaurants, picking those he felt would complement his ambition to explore new territory food-wise while enhancing his credentials among his peers. Yet he also needed to be reminded of the important part classical French cookery played in the history of British cuisine and during a spell at and Manley's restaurant in West Sussex as a sous chef (this restaurant had a Michelin Star and four AA rosettes), the chef proprietor Karl Loderer provided this. But, despite this growing fund of knowledge, Peter was finding it difficult to know what direction it was best to take next. Then a phone call came from his old friend Michael Collom, Head Chef at The Priory: 'Peter, you need to stop fannying around – it's time you became a Head Chef and I know just the people for you.'

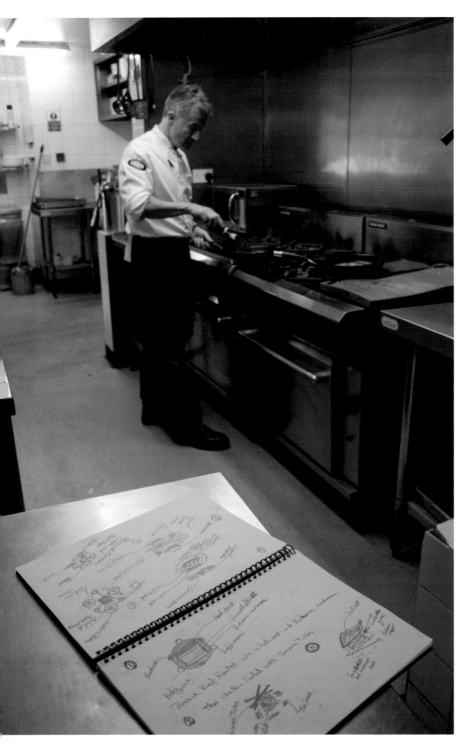

Elaine and Ian Gatehouse had recently purchased The Horn of Plenty Hotel and Restaurant deep in the heart of the Devon countryside and they invited Peter down to look around. 'Sonia Stevenson had previously been chef proprietor there and had built up an enviable reputation, gaining a Michelin Star. She would be a hard act to follow and I knew the media would be on my case, but with the support and enthusiasm of the Gatehouses I thought I could make it work. As it happened my dreams were almost shattered by a spiteful review in the press – completely unreasonable as I was cooking the same food as I had at Manley's. But then Martin Greaves, an Egon Ronay Inspector, came to our rescue and wrote a fantastic review saying "The food here speaks for itself". This was a lesson in the power of the media – and also an eye-opener in to how the food press works.'

Over the following years The Horn of Plenty went from strength to strength and accolades were showered upon it, winning Hotel of the Year and Best Lunch in Britain awards, gaining a Michelin Star and 3 AA Rosettes, with consistently high marks in every national food guide. TV interest followed, first with a Westcountry TV programme 'Compliments to the Chef' and then 'Peter Gorton for Starters' which was shortlisted for a Programme of the Year Award. Peter had a second series commissioned 'Peter Cooking Away' This was the dawn of the age of the celebrity chef and Peter was one of the first to be chosen, not least for his infectious smile and obvious enthusiasm for his work. He also made a TV series called 'Little Chefs', programmes devoted to children and cooking – a theme that has remained close to Peter's heart. Peter also featured in the programme 'Kill it, Cook it, Eat it'.

In 1996 Peter published his first book *Peter Gorton's Horn of Plenty Cookery Book*. Peter was looking to move on to his own restaurant but entrepreneur Paul Roston came on the scene having purchased The Horn of Plenty and, for a time, Peter agreed to continue as Head Chef.

At this time one of the country's headlining provincial restaurants was The Carved Angel in Dartmouth. Here Joyce Molyneaux presided as one of Britain's finest women chefs over more than two decades. The restaurant was now on the market and Paul and Peter decided to purchase it and go into business together. While continuing to grow The Carved Angel's reputation, Peter found himself removed from his first love, cooking, into dealing with the administration of by now a chain of restaurants and cafés all over the Westcountry and also the

but grew into a restaurant through the demand of its customers. Here Peter can fulfil his ambitions as a chef, working with a small team to produce the sort of food that is created out of his accumulated years of experience. From here Peter intends to expand his interests in other aspects of food and catering, acting as advisor to a variety of organisations, establishing a cookery school, organising a Food Fair and acting as an ambassador for Westcountry food producers, as championed in his recently published book *Devon Food Heroes*.

It is when Peter discusses his work with schools that his passion for food shines through with particular fierceness. 'I truly believe that we need to start educating our children as young as possible about food, the importance of eating healthily, and issues regarding food security and population growth. We are putting so much pressure on the earth's resources that we are jeopardising our children's futures. It's too late to start this kind of teaching at secondary level, by that time the habits of poor eating relating to obesity are ingrained. I love talking to primary school children about food – they share my enthusiasm and when I tell them that "Food Should be Fun" they really know what I'm talking about.'

evolving 'Carved Angel Christmas Pudding Company', so with all this it brought a complete stop to any chance of being in the kitchen full time: 'I found it increasingly frustrating,' Peter recalled. 'I had become a fixer rather than a creator – it was simply not what I wanted to do.

Once again it was time to move on.' Peter and Paul were able to do this when they sold all The Carved Angels restaurants and lastly 'The Horn of Plenty' in 2010. Paul went on to grow 'The Carved Angel Christmas Pudding Company' and Peter went on to open his own restaurant, Gorton's.

Gorton's is what might be described as a bespoke restaurant sited in the heart of Tavistock, one of Devon's oldest market towns. Gorton's was purchased in 2011 and was originally intended as a dining club

Peter believes we're in danger of losing our sense of family. 'The French and Italians have got it right and I'd like to get back to a time when families come together around the table, when food becomes the focus and through which we communicate with each other.'

Family is clearly at the heart of Peter's life. Almost certainly his own childhood, the loss of his mother and the fracturing of his relationship with his father, strengthened his resolve to create a strong foundation for his own family. 'I swore to myself early on that if I ever had a family I would invest time in them.' He laughs '"Food and Family" – that could be my epitaph!'

Simon Butler
Halsgrove

Peter at home with the family.

# Fish and Shellfish

# Terrine of Smoked Salmon with Sautéed Scallops and Sauce Vierge

...................................................................

**Ingredients – Serves 16 portions of terrine**
175g unsalted butter
Zest of ½ a lemon, finely grated
Juice ½ lemon
2 tablespoons chopped flat leaf parsley
1 tablespoon chopped chives
Salt and pepper to taste
800g long cut smoked salmon

**Method**
Line a 1kg terrine or bread tin with cling film allowing a slight overhang.  Mix the butter in a food processor until light and airy.  Add the lemon juice, herbs and salt and pepper to taste.

Cover the base of the terrine with a layer of smoked salmon with a palette knife, covering the entire surface continue to build the terrine with alternating layers of smoked salmon and  butter mixture until all the ingredients have been used or the terrine is full.  Finish with a layer of smoked salmon.

Cover the top of the terrine with the overhang of cling film.  Refrigerate overnight to allow the butter to set.

Turn out the terrine on to a clean chopping board and slice with a sharp knife into the desired portion size.

**Scallops – Serves 4**
12 hand-caught scallops
2 tablespoons sunflower oil
Salt and freshly ground pepper to taste

**Method**
Heat a heavy duty frying pan, add the oil and put the scallops in the pan, sear the scallops for 60 seconds, turn over then sear on the other side for 45 seconds.  Remove the scallops on to a clean tray and keep warm

**Sauce Vierge – Serves 4**
12ml olive oil
1 tablespoon balsamic vinegar
2 plum tomatoes, skins and seeds removed,
    flesh diced into concassé
1 shallot peeled and finely chopped
1 small garlic clove, peeled and finely chopped
2 tablespoons chopped fresh basil
2 tablespoons chopped fresh chives

**Method**
Pour the olive oil in a bowl and add the balsamic vinegar and whisk.  Add the rest of the ingredients and mix well.  Season with salt and pepper and set aside for the flavours to infuse with each other for about 20 minutes.

**To serve**
On four cold starter plates, place a nice pile of dressed salad leaves in the centre, add three slices of the terrine and 3 scallops and lastly sprinkle a little sauce vierge.

Brill Wrapped in
Parma Ham with
Sicilian Pesto
and Creamy
Garlic
Polenta

**Ingredients – Serves 4**
4 brill fillets
4 thin slices Parma ham
Salt and freshly ground black pepper

**Method**
**Pre-heat oven to 230°c/fan oven 210°c/ gas 8**
Season the brill fillets lightly and wrap with the Parma ham.

Heat some oil in an oven-proof frying pan. Put the brill into the pan and seal for 20 seconds, turn the fillets over and place in the oven and leave to cook for 3 minutes, remove from the oven and keep warm.

**Creamy Polenta**
**Ingredients – Serves 6**
1 tablespoon unsalted butter
1 tablespoon olive oil
2 teaspoons of minced garlic
335ml full cream milk
335ml double cream
335ml water
1 bay leaf
58g polenta (yellow cornmeal)
50g Parmesan cheese, freshly grated
Salt and pepper

**Method**
In a heavy bottomed saucepan melt the butter over medium heat. Add the oil and garlic, sweat garlic for 2 minutes without browning. Add the cream, milk and water to the pan and increase the heat to high and add the bay leaf, simmer for 5 minutes then remove the bay leaf.

Whisking constantly pour the cornmeal into the boiling liquid in a thin stream; cook stirring with a wooden spoon until the polenta begins to thicken. Stir in the cheese and pour the polenta out into a baking tray.

**Sicilian Pesto**
**Ingredients**
2 cloves garlic, peeled
Large handful of leaves basil
1 tablespoon of celery leaves
100 g blanched almonds, roughly chopped or pine nuts
4 sun dried tomatoes, peeled and chopped
6 tablespoon olive oil
Salt and freshly ground black pepper

**Method**
In a mortar pound the garlic and basil into a paste.
Add the almonds, little by little, pounding after each addition, then the tomatoes. When all the ingredients are reduced to a pulp, add the olive oil and the salt and pepper. Alternately use an electric blender, in which case the oil should be added at the beginning.

# Lightly Smoked Mackerel with Pumpkin Seed and Tomato and Rosemary Flavoured Dressing

.....................................

## Ingredients – Serves 4
200g rice
2 sprigs of rosemary
4 cloves of garlic, peeled and left whole
2 medium sized very fresh mackerel, filleted
Olive oil
2 tablespoons lightly roasted pumpkin seeds
100g Greek feta cheese
2 x handfuls of mixed salad leaves

## Method
Line a wok with two sheets of foil, add rice and cover with a sprig of rosemary saving a little for later. Sprinkle with a little water and heat over a medium heat until smoking, place lightly oiled mackerel fillets on a wire rack in the base of the wok, cover and smoke for 2-3 minutes, remove from the heat.

Heat a heavy frying pan until hot, brush fillets with olive oil and season to taste then cook over a high heat for 1-2 minutes on each side until well browned, keep warm.

## Sweet potato blinis
200g sweet potatoes
85g plain flour
1 egg
3 tablespoons natural full fat yoghurt
Sunflower oil
Salt and freshly ground black pepper

## Method
Cook the sweet potatoes in plenty of boiling water, when they are very tender, peel them and mash to a fine purée. Cool and while slightly lukewarm mix in the flour and egg, season with salt and pepper. Add a tablespoon of the natural yoghurt one at a time to achieve a thick pancake batter consistency.

Heat a lightly oiled non-stick frying pan and when hot add spoonsful of the batter sufficient to make a nice size blini. Brown lightly on both sides and keep warm.

## Tomato Dressing
3 cloves garlic chopped roughly
2 shallots, chopped roughly
5 plum tomatoes with the seeds removed
300ml tomato juice
2 tablespoons white wine vinegar
2 pinches of sugar
Sprigs of rosemary
Salt and pepper to taste
150ml olive oil

## Method
Heat a small saucepan and add some olive oil and cook the garlic and shallot until soft, add the plum tomatoes and cook for 1 minute add the white wine vinegar and allow to cook for 30 seconds then add the sugar and tomato juice continue to cook for 3 minutes finally adding the rosemary sprig.

Remove from the heat and cover with cling film for two hours to allow the flavours to infuse. When cold, sieve the dressing through a fine sieve and refrigerate.

## To Serve
Combine some mixed salad leaves, pumpkin seeds, feta cheese in a bowl and coat with a little tomato dressing. Divide the sweet potato blinis between 4 starter plates, place a little salad on top of each blini and top with a mackerel fillet and serve.

**Smoked Salmon Mousse with Pickled Cucumber Salad, Tomato Jelly and a Chive Cream**

## Ingredients – Serves 6

### Mousse
140g smoked salmon
50ml Noilly Prat vermouth
2 leaves gelatine, soaked in cold water
Lemon juice
225ml whipping cream, beaten to the ribbon stage
50ml sour cream
1 teaspoon horseradish cream (optional)

### Method
Have ready six ramekins 6 cm x 5 cm deep.  Brush the insides of ramekins with olive oil.  In a food processor cut the smoked salmon to a fine paste or purée.  Refrigerate.

Pour the Noilly prat into a shallow pan with the fish stock and reduce by half, add the gelatine and remove from the stove, allow to cool. Beat up the whipping cream to a ribbon stage, set aside.

Add the fish stock and gelatine reduction to the smoked salmon purée and process until well mixed.  Add lemon juice to taste.  Fold in the sour cream and whipping cream and pour into the ramekins and chill in a refrigerator for at least 4 hours.

### Pickled Cucumbers
1 cucumber cut in half lengthways
60ml rice wine vinegar
1 bay leaf
100g sugar
½ thinly sliced red onion
Salt and pepper
60g thinly sliced fennel (optional)

### Method
Scrape the seeds from the cucumber, discard the seeds and shave the cucumber into long strips with a vegetable peeler or slicer. Place the bay leaves, vinegar, sugar and chilli in a saucepan and simmer for 5 minutes.  Strain and cool.

Combine the cucumbers, onion, fennel, salt and pepper and cooled vinegar mixture and refrigerate for at least 3 hours.
These cucumbers will keep in the refrigerator for up to one week.

### Tomato Jelly
600g ripe tomatoes
200ml fish stock
200ml passata
3 egg whites
1 small leek, finely chopped
½ tablespoon Pernod
1 tablespoon white wine vinegar
5 sheets gelatine, soaked in cold water

### Method
Cut the tomatoes into small pieces and process in a blender until smooth.  Pass through a fine mesh sieve, mix with the fish stock, passata and egg whites, and bring the chopped leek, Pernod and white wine vinegar to the boil in a saucepan, bring up to a boil then turn down to a simmer and cook for 20 minutes, make a little hole in the egg whites to allow the steam to be released.

When the tomato stock looks clear remove it from the heat and pass through a muslin cloth in a strainer and add the soaked gelatine.  Mix well and allow to cool.  Pour on top of the smoked salmon mousse, return to the fridge until set

### Chive Cream
250ml whipping cream
85g horseradish cream
25g Dijon mustard
140g natural yoghurt
 55g chives, finely chopped
Juice of 1 lemon
Salt and cayenne pepper

**liquidise all these ingredients
and strain through a fine sieve,
it will keep for 3 days**

### To Serve
Turn out the mousses in the centre of each plate, top each mousse with some pickled cucumber and mixed tiny salad leaves.

# Pan-Fried Squid with Belly Pork and a Sweet Pepper Ragout

..........................................................

## Ingredients – Serves 6
800g belly pork
1 level tablespoon five spice
Salt
Freshly ground black pepper
6 cloves of garlic
3 star anise
Sunflower oil

## Method
**Pre-heat the oven to 110°c/ fan oven 80°c/gas ¼**
Place the belly pork fat side down on a tray and rub the meat side with five spice, salt and pepper. Cover and leave in the fridge overnight.

Line a roasting tray with baking paper and place the pork fat side down on to the roasting tray. Add the garlic, star anise, and enough oil to just cover the pork. Cover with another piece of baking paper and then cover with tinfoil. Place in the oven for 12 hours.

Once cooked, lift the pork gently from the roasting tin and place on to a tray lined with baking paper. Put another sheet of baking paper on top of the pork then another tray, wrap tightly with cling film and put in the fridge with a weight on top evenly distributed over the tray and leave overnight to press.

**Pre-heat the oven to 230°c/ fan oven 210°c/gas 8**
Unwrap the pork and place on a chopping board. Trim the sides to create an even shape and then cut 12 squares of pork. Heat a little sunflower oil in an oven proof frying pan, then add the pork, fat side down, and place in the oven for about 8 minutes, or until the fat goes crispy . Remove pan from the oven, turn the pork over so the fat side is facing upwards and baste over a medium heat until the pork is nicely caramelised.

## Sweet Pepper Ragout
1 red and 1 yellow pepper, cored, seeded and diced
50ml olive oil
1 onion chopped finely
4 cloves of garlic, crushed and chopped finely
Pinch of cayenne pepper
1 tablespoon fresh herbs, parsley and basil
225ml passata
125ml dry white wine
Salt and freshly ground white pepper

## Method
In heavy sauce pan, heat 50ml of olive oil, sauté the onion, garlic and cayenne pepper together for 5 minutes. Stir in the tomatoes, peppers and saffron.

Pour in the white wine and reduce by half over a medium heat until all the liquid is absorbed. Add the passata and cook for 15 minutes, season and add the fresh herbs. Keep warm.

## Squid
2 medium squid cleaned
1 teaspoon sea salt
½ teaspoon freshly ground black pepper
2 tablespoons plain flour
2 tablespoon sunflower oil

## Method
Cut squid into strips, toss in a little flour and make sure you remove excess flour, set aside.
Heat a large sauté pan, add the oil and the squid, cook for 1 minute then remove to a plate and keep warm.

**To serve** - Place 1/2 tablespoon of ragout on a plate and assemble the pork and squid.

# Oriental Style Mussels

## Ingredients – Serves 4

1kg fresh live Mussels
15g butter
1 stick lemon grass/crushed
10g chopped shallots
100ml white wine
10g chopped garlic
Juice of 1 lime
3 fresh chillis
6 large tomatoes, skinned and diced
400ml tin coconut milk
10g chopped ginger
20ml olive oil
Chopped coriander – to taste
Chopped basil – to taste

## Method

Wash, clean and de-beard the mussels, discarding any that stay open.  Sauté the shallots, garlic, ginger and chilli in the olive oil.  Add the crushed lemon grass and mussels to the pan and pour in the white wine, place a lid on the pan and cook and shake the pan until all the mussels have opened.

Add the tin of coconut milk and cook for one minute to heat through, add the tomatoes, lime juice and chopped coriander and basil.  Finally pour into a serving dish with fresh crusty bread on side.

# Crab Crusted Wild Sea Bass and a Laurier Dressing

........................................................

### Ingredients – Serves 6
6 x 160g wild sea bass fillets, skin off
55g fresh breadcrumbs
30g parsley and mixed fresh herbs
80g butter
25g Gruyère
100g white crab meat

### Method
Place the breadcrumbs and herbs into a food processor and mix until the herbs are finally chopped and the breadcrumbs have turned green in colour. Add the butter and the cheese, continue to process until all the ingredients are fully combined. Add the crabmeat and pulse the food processor to just mix in the crab.

Empty the mixture on to a sheet of baking paper. Form into a ball with your hands, top with another sheet of paper and using a rolling pin roll to about four millimetres in thickness, chill.

### Cooking the Fish
**Pre-heat oven to 220°c**
Season fish fillets with salt. Remove the crab crust from the fridge. Take off the top layer of paper and cut rectangles of crab crust the some size as your fish portions. Place on top of the fish, put on to buttered baking paper in an ovenproof frying pan and cook in the oven for about 6 to 8 minutes. Remove fish from the oven and allow to rest for 3 minutes.

### Laurier Dressing
**Ingredients**
2 shallots
2 cloves minced garlic
6 tablespoon olive oil
350ml cups dry white wine
2 fresh bay leaves torn to release their oils
2 tablespoon fresh lemon juice
1 tablespoon balsamic vinegar
175ml tomato passata
Salt and freshly ground pepper
4 tablespoon softened butter (optional)

### Method
Place the shallots, garlic and olive oil into a small saucepan over a low heat for 2 minutes, stirring occasionally. Add the balsamic vinegar, white wine and bay leaves. Increase the heat and cook and reduce by half.

Add the tomato passata, lemon juice, salt and pepper. Bring the mixture to the boil and remove from the heat. Remove the bay leaves and slowly whisk in the softened butter. Adjust the seasoning. Serve with potato gnocchi.

**Chef's Tip**

*This crust recipe works very well with salmon, brill and farmed sea bass and is also nice on a breast of chicken. The crust recipe can be cut into the desired shape to top any fish or chicken and frozen until needed.*

# Pan-Fried Gilthead Bream on a Spiced Aubergine and a Pea Pancake

**Ingredients Serves – 4 (Starter size)**
4 x 50g fillets of gilthead bream
2 tablespoons of sunflower oil
Sea salt and freshly ground black pepper

**Method**
Heat a heavy duty frying pan. Add the sunflower oil and place the guilthead bream fillets in the pan and sear until the skin is crispy. Turn and cook for 1 minute or until the fish is just cooked.

### Pea Pancakes

225g peas – fresh or frozen cooked until tender
1 whole egg + 1 egg yolk
112ml double cream
3 tablespoons plain flour
2 tablespoons butter
Salt and freshly ground black pepper

### Method

Drain the peas and in a food processor combine the peas, egg yolk, cream, and flour until a smooth batter. Refrigerate until required. Melt the butter in a sauté pan. Place 1 tablespoon of batter for each pancake in the pan and cook on both sides until the edges are brown. Drain on kitchen paper and keep warm.

### Lightly Spiced Aubergine Purée

500g fresh aubergines
2 tablespoons sun-dried tomatoes
1 small onion and finely diced about 50g
2 Spring onions, chopped
1 finely diced cloves of garlic
Ground cumin to taste
1 small bunch of fresh coriander finely chopped
1 teaspoon of honey

### Method

Cut the aubergines in half lengthwise, brush with olive oil, lie on a baking sheet and roast for 30 minutes, remove from the oven and cool. When cool, scoop the pulp away from the skin, discard the skin, heat the olive oil in a large frying pan and sauté the onions until translucent. Add the garlic and continue to cook for one minute more. Do not allow the garlic to brown. Add the cumin, honey and salt and pepper, mix well and set aside to cool. Add the spring onions and coriander, place in a container until ready to use.

### To Serve

Put a warm pea pancake in the centre of a pre-heated dinner plate, place a spoon of aubergine purée on top and then the gilthead bream and serve.

### Chef's Tip

*The gilthead bream is generally considered the best tasting of the breams. This spiced aubergine purée is a wonderful addition for vegetarian recipes also it complements lamb dishes.*

# Sautéed Scallops with Coriander Puy Lentils and a Coconut Sauce

........................................................

### Ingredients – Serves 4
12 hand-caught scallops, white meat only
2 tablespoons of sunflower oil
Sea salt and freshly ground black pepper

### Method
Heat a heavy duty frying pan. Add the sunflower oil, put in the scallops and sear for 30 seconds. Turn once and sear for another 30 seconds then remove on to a clean tray and keep warm.

### Coriander Lentils
300g puy lentils
250g chicken stock or vegetable stock
50g unsalted butter
2 spring onions, finely sliced
2 tablespoons chopped coriander

### Method
Place the puy lentils in a medium saucepan, cover with water and bring to a simmer, cook lentils for about 10 minutes or until they are soft to bite but still keeping their form, drain and allow to steam dry. Place lentils and remaining ingredients into a saucepan and bring to a boil. Cook the lentils in the stock until all the stock has reduced. Keep warm.

### Pickled Cucumbers
½ a melon cut into small cubes
½ cucumber seeds removed
200ml rice wine vinegar
60g sugar
2 star anise
1 bay leaf

### Method
Peel the cucumber and cut it into small cubes, heat the vinegar and dissolve the sugar in it . Add the star anise and the torn bay leaf and allow this to infuse for 30 minutes. When cool add the cucumber cubes, leave the mixture to marinate for 6 hours. Take the cucumber out of the marinade and leave it to drain in a strainer.

### Coconut Sauce
100ml double cream
600ml chicken stock or fish stock
1 sprig thyme
15g coconut paste
200ml coconut milk
1 teaspoon chopped ginger fine
Juice of 1 lime optional
50g butter

### Method
Gently boil the cream until reduced to half the quantity. Similarly the chicken stock with the thyme should also be reduced to half the quantity. Strain the chicken stock and add the cream, coconut paste and coconut milk. Gently boil this sauce for 5 minutes, remove from the heat and stir in the knobs of butter.

### To serve
Place 3 tablespoons of puy lentils on pre-heated plates, place a scallop on each and arrange the melon and cucumber around , finally whip up the coconut sauce to a froth with a hand blender and pour around the scallops and serve.

# Lightly Spiced Lemon Grass and Seafood Broth

**Ingredients – Serves 4**
**Stage 1 for the broth**
3 tablespoons peanut oil
2 sticks of chopped lemongrass
6 chopped kaffir lime leaves
30g peeled chopped ginger
4 red Thai chillies, finely chopped
4 cloves of garlic, peeled and crushed
½ a small onion finely chopped
1 stick chopped celery
1 small chopped carrot
2 litres cold water
50g palm sugar (Asian food stores)
Limejuice to taste

**Stage 2**
Fish sauce to taste
340ml passata
4 scallops pan-fried (optional)
100g king prawns
100g mussels
Canned coconut milk to taste
30g snow peas blanched and thinly sliced
2 tomatoes, concassé (optional)
4 spring onions, finely chopped
Small handful of picked basil leaves, coriander leaves roughly chopped

**Method**
**Stage 1**
Heat the peanut oil in a stockpot on a medium high heat. Add the garlic, lemon grass, kaffir lime leaves, ginger, chillies, onions, celery and carrots.

Sauté for 5 minutes or until the onions are soft and translucent. Add water, palm sugar, fish sauce and limejuice.

Bring to the boil for 2 minutes then remove from the heat and leave for 20 minutes then strain through a fine mesh sieve, discard solids and reserve the broth.

**Stage 2**
**To assemble**
Re-heat the broth in a medium saucepan. Add the coconut milk to taste, cook for 2 minutes. Season with salt and pepper.

Add the scallops (optional) king prawns and mussels until nicely cooked then add the snow peas, fresh herbs, spring onions and tomato concassé. Serve in the large bowls.

> ### Chef's Tip
> *I also like to add noodles to this recipe, it has a*
> *very clean taste and my children love it!*

# Meat, Game and Poultry

# Roast Loin of Venison with a Tangle of Greens and Red Wine Shallots

**Ingredients – Serves 6**
6 x 140g trimmed venison loin
Salt and freshly ground black pepper
2 tablespoons grapeseed oil

**Cooking the venison**
**Pre-heat the oven 230°c/fan oven 210°c/gas 8**
Heat the grapeseed oil in a frying pan and when hot add the venison. Seal the venison on all the sides and put on to a baking tray, season with salt and pepper and cook in the oven for six minutes (medium rare). Remove from the oven and let the venison rest for five minutes.

**Tangle of Tart Greens**
**Ingredients**
½ head of a small Savoy cabbage
2 rashers of smoked bacon
½ red onion, thinly sliced
1 bunch watercress, coarse stems removed
1 bunch of baby spinach
1 tablespoon sugar
2-3 tablespoons balsamic vinegar/or red wine vinegar
Salt and freshly ground pepper to taste

**Method**
Core and coarsely shred the cabbage with a sharp knife. In a 10-inch saucepan sauté the bacon over a medium heat. Add the onion and cabbage and sauté until the cabbage begins to wilt. Add the sugar and vinegar and cook until the cabbage is tender but still a little crisp. Remove the saucepan from the heat, toss in the watercress and season to taste. Serve warm.

Red wine Shallots (see page 134)

**Butternut Squash Purée – makes 500ml**
1 onion, finely sliced
Grapeseed oil
500g chopped butternut squash
3 tablespoons butter, unsalted
Salt and pepper to taste

**Pre-heat the oven to 200°c/fan oven 180°c/gas 6**
Sauté the onions in a little grapeseed oil without colouring them until soft. Place in a small roasting tray with remaining ingredients, add a splash of water. Cover the tray with tinfoil and pierce a few holes to let the steam to escape, place in the oven until the butternut squash is soft.

Place the butternut squash in a food processor and process to a smooth purée with the unsalted butter, check the seasoning and keep warm.

**To Serve**
Now place two tablespoons of the tangle of greens on a plate spoon a line of butternut purée on the plate. Slice venison on top of the tangle of greens, place two red wine shallots on the plate and spoon a nice red wine sauce over and around the venison.

# Roasted Woodpigeon on a Butternut and Smoked Bacon Squash Risotto

....................................................

**Ingredients – Serves 4–6/starter portion**
2 whole wood pigeon
2 tablespoon grapeseed oil
Salt and freshly ground pepper

**Method**

**Pre-heat the oven 220°c/fan oven 200°c/gas 7**
In a heavy frying pan, seal the pigeon until brown, season and roast in the oven for 10 minutes. Remove from the oven and place on a resting rack for 5 minutes.

**Caramelised Squash**
3 tablespoons grapeseed oil
1 large 900g butternut squash, peeled and cut into ¾ inch cubes
Course salt and freshly ground pepper
2 teaspoons light brown sugar

**Method**
In a large sauté pan, heat the grapeseed oil until hot. Season the squash with salt and pepper add it to the pan and cook, stirring occasionally until nicely browned, about 6 minutes. Cook and cover until tender, about 5 minutes. Add the brown sugar and cook until the squash is caramelized, but still holding its shape, about 2 minutes then set aside.

**Risotto**
2 litres vegetable or chicken stock
2 tablespoons olive oil
50g lightly smoked streaky bacon, cut into ½ inch dice

225g finely chopped shallots
300g Italian rice (Arborio etc.)
1 teaspoon fresh sage chopped
¼ teaspoon fresh thyme leaves
125ml dry white wine
Coarse sea salt and freshly ground pepper to taste
50g grated parmesan (optional)

**Method**
In a large saucepan, bring the stock to a boil over a high heat. Reduce the heat and keep hot. In a large heavy bottomed saucepan, heat the oil over a medium heat. Add the bacon and cook until lightly browned, about 5 minutes. Add the shallots and cook, stirring often, until softened, about 3 minutes.

Reduce the heat to medium-low. Stir in the rice, sage and thyme. Cook, stirring with a wooden spoon, until the rice is coated and has started to release its starch and turns a milky opaque white and begins to stick to the bottom of the pan, about 5 minutes. Add the wine and boil until completely reduced, about 2–3 minutes. Ladle about 225ml of the simmering stock into the rice, cook, stirring often, until the stock is almost completely absorbed by the rice.

Continue cooking and stirring, adding another 225ml of stock. After 15 minutes, begin tasting the rice. At this point, add the remaining stock, judiciously. The rice should be firm, yet cooked through. Add the caramelized butternut squash to the risotto, check seasoning and place in the centre of 4 heated bowls, slice your pigeon breast on top.

# Marinated Beef Salad with a Chilli Mango Salsa

**Ingredients – Serves 4 – this is a starter portion**
**Miso Marinade**
1 tablespoon red miso or hoisin sauce
2 tablespoons plus 1½ teaspoons sugar
¼ teaspoon grated fresh ginger
¼ teaspoon grated fresh garlic
1 tablespoon Asian toasted sesame oil
½ teaspoon soy sauce
1 tablespoon dry sherry
(1 x 12oz steak fillet or sirloin) cut into 4 thin steaks

**Method**
**Miso Marinade**
Whisk together all the ingredients in a medium bowl. Add the steak, cover and marinate for 1 hour in the refrigerator turning twice. Marinate up to 24 hours.

**Chilli mango salsa**
1 large mango ripe but firm
1 small red pepper, finely diced
1 small Spanish onion, medium dice
1 clove garlic
1 bird's eye chilli finely minced
Juice of 1 lime
1 tablespoon basil
Salt & pepper

**Mango salsa**
Cut the mango flesh into 1cm/½ inch dice. Roast the red peppers peel then dice and add to the mango also chopped onion, garlic, chilli, lime juice and chopped basil. Very gently mix all the ingredients together and add freshly grated salt and black pepper, refrigerate for at least an hour.

**Vegetable Salad**
1 iceberg lettuce
¼ cucumber peeled and deseeded
1 carrot
2 tablespoons thinly sliced onion
French beans, steamed and blanched
2 plum tomato, peeled seeded and diced

**Vegetable Salad**
Combine the cucumber, carrot, red onion, French beans, and tomatoes, set aside.

**To Cook the Steak**
Remove the steak slices from the marinade, grill the steak for about 1 minute per side for medium rare cut the steak into strips about ¼ inch by 3 inches long. Add the steak to the salad and toss with the vinaigrette.

**To Serve**
Take two iceberg leaves and set them together on a starter plate then place steak and vegetables on them, sprinkle with fresh herbs and pour dressing around.

# Thai Chicken Salad

**Ingredients – Serves 4**
4 x chicken breasts (with skin on) or pre-cooked turkey, beef, goose
leftovers
Half a cucumber – seed and cut into slices
2 fresh chillies - seeded and cut into fine strips
6 small shallots sliced thinly
I large tablespoon of ginger finely chopped
2 cloves of garlic finely chopped
55g chopped coriander

50ml lime juice
3 tablespoons fish sauce
2 tablespoons sugar
½ tablespoon salt
3 tablespoons grapeseed oil
55g chopped roasted peanuts/optional
Iceberg lettuce or baby gem
Bunch of spring onions, chopped finely

**Method**
Add the chicken breasts to a saucepan of boiling water then reduce
the heat and simmer for 8 minutes. Take off the heat and let chicken
rest in the cooking water for 20 minutes. Remove the chicken and
discard the skin. With your hands pull the meat apart in shreds, about
1.5 inches long, set aside.

De-seed the cucumber, cut into slices and add to the chicken. In
another bowl add the chillies, shallots, ginger and garlic, toss with lime
juice, grapeseed oil, fish sauce and other ingredients then add to the
chicken and cucumber and mix thoroughly, stir in the coriander. Place
on top of crisp iceberg lettuce, sprinkle with chopped peanuts and
serve.

*When I was working in Bangkok, I would eat this salad a couple of times a week; it is definitely one of my favourite salads, full of fresh flavours*

# Roasted Partridge with Braised Red Cabbage and Wild Rice Pancake

## Ingredients
4 young partridges about 250g each in weight
2 tablespoons grapeseed oil
Salt and ground white pepper
2 rashers or smoked bacon (optional)

## Method
### Pre-heat oven 220°c/fan oven 200°c/gas 7
In a large frying pan heat the butter and oil and brown the partridges for 2 minutes on each thigh and 30 seconds on each breast. Turn them on their backs and place half a rasher of smoked bacon on top of each pigeons and roast for 12-15 minutes. Pour off the fat and leave to rest for a few minutes in a warm place, covered with greaseproof paper and keep warm.

### Wild Rice Pancakes – Makes about 15 pancakes
1 tablespoon chopped spring onions
2 teaspoon grapeseed oil
1 teaspoon butter
1 egg
1 egg yolk
1 teaspoon of cumin
225ml milk
225g plain flour
1 tablespoon baking powder
350g cooked wild rice
1 tablespoon of fresh herbs, optional
Oil for cooking

### Wild Rice Pancakes
Sauté the spring onions in grapeseed oil for 2 minutes, place the egg, egg yolk and milk in a medium bowl and whisk until well blended. Sift together the flour and baking powder add the egg mixture and whisk until smooth. Fold in the wild rice, herbs etc.

### Cooking the Pancakes
Heat two tablespoons of grapeseed oil in a pan and place one good heaped tablespoon of wild rice pancake mixture into the oil to form a 5cms/2-inch pancake. Repeat four times. Cook for one minute then flip over and cook on the other side for two minutes more. Remove from the pan and set aside and keep warm.

### Braised Red Cabbage (see page 74)

### To serve
Place a wild rice pancake in the centre of each plate and arrange one tablespoon of braised red cabbage on the pancakes. Carve the partridge breasts and place on top. Pour a red wine sauce over and around the partridge and serve.

> ## Chef's Tips
> *If your game bird is young and in prime condition then the best thing is simply to roast it with a good sauce as an accompaniment.*
>
> *There are two varieties of partridges, the English grey-leg and the French red-legged which is bigger than the English grey-leg. The partridge season is 1st September to 1st February.*

# Braised Duck with Lemon Grass, Ginger and Soy, Asparagus and Shitake Mushroom Stir-Fry

.........................................................

**Ingredients – Serves 6**
2 ducks
720ml chicken stock
2 tablespoon chopped, fresh lemongrass
1 tablespoon finely chopped, fresh ginger
2 tablespoon sun dried tomatoes
1 tablespoon dried thyme
2 tablespoons sherry
3 tablespoons soy sauce
3 tablespoons apple or fruit jelly
2 large sprigs fresh rosemary
Salt and pepper
2 tablespoons of fresh chopped coriander

**Method**
**Pre-heat the oven - 150°c/fan oven 130°c/gas 2**
Cut up the duck and brown well in a pan. Transfer the pieces to a casserole. Combine the rest of the ingredients and bring to the boil, pour over the duck, cover and cook in the oven for 1½ hours.

Remove the duck from the liquid, set aside covered. Put the liquid in the fridge and when it is cool, remove the fat from the surface. Reheat the duck in the sauce, and season to taste.

**Asparagus and Shitake Mushroom Stir-Fry**
2 cloves of garlic, crushed
12 shitake mushrooms, thinly sliced
12 asparagus spears, thinly sliced
1 teaspoon finely chopped ginger
2 plum tomatoes, concassé (see page 136)
Salt and freshly ground pepper

**Method**
Heat a little grapeseed oil in a wok and when hot add crushed garlic and cook for 15 seconds. Add the shitake mushrooms and asparagus and continue to cook for one minute. Add the ginger and tomato concassé for another minute, tossing the vegetables well. Remove from the heat and keep warm.

**To Serve**
Place a few tablespoons of asparagus and shitake stir-fry in the centre of four heated dinner plates, arrange the duck pieces around and pour over the reduced sauce and serve with a good sprinkling of chopped coriander.

# Roast Guinea Fowl Marinated in Cumin, Garlic and Lime with Potato Knish and Sweet and Sour Leeks

....................................................

### Ingredients – Serves 4
4 guinea fowl breasts or 2 whole pheasants
4 tablespoons cumin
2 tablespoons minced garlic
1 teaspoon chopped sage
2 tablespoon ground allspice
1 teaspoon ground ginger
2 tablespoon salt to taste
175ml lime juice
¼ cup olive oil

### Method
In a bowl combine the seasoning, lime juice and olive oil. Rub the mixture over the Guinea fowl breasts, cover and refrigerate overnight. Pre-heat the oven to 220°c/fan oven 200°c/gas 7.
In a hot pan place the breasts, skin-side down to colour and when golden, turn and seal the other side until brown. Place skin side down on a tray and bake the Guinea fowl breasts for 10 minutes basting a couple of times with the juices, set aside and allow to rest for 5 minutes.

### Potato Knish – Serves 4-6
**Pre-heat oven to gas 5/375°f/190°c**
4 large potatoes pricked with a fork
4 tablespoons chopped chives
4 tablespoons fresh coriander
2 tablespoons olive oil
Salt and pepper
3 sheets filo pastry
115g clarified butter

### Method
Bake the potatoes for about an hour until tender. When cool enough to handle, peel and place the flesh in a medium bowl. Add a little olive oil and lightly crush the potatoes, allow to cool. Then add fresh herbs season with salt and pepper and set aside.

Butter one sheet of filo pastry with the clarified butter then repeat with the second one, place on top of one another, place the potato in a long strip on the long side of the rectangle and roll up like a sausage roll. Place in the fridge to firm up, when needed cut into four equal portions and place in a hot oven until golden brown and crispy.

### Sweet and Sour Leeks
1kg leeks
2 cloves of garlic
1 tablespoon sugar
4 tablespoons olive oil
Juice of 1 lemon
1 tablespoon soy sauce (optional)

### Method
Clean the leeks thoroughly. Cut off the tough green part. Cut the leeks into longish slices. Fry the crushed garlic and sugar in hot oil until the sugar caramelises slightly. Add the leeks and turn them a little over moderate heat. Sprinkle with lemon juice. Cover and stew gently over a low heat until tender. Serve hot or cold.

### To Serve
Place a good heaped tablespoon of sweet and sour leeks on 4 pre-heated dinner plates, slice the guinea fowl on top of the leeks. Place a potato knish on the plate and serve with a sauce of your choice.

> ## Chef's Tip
> *This marinade is suitable with any game bird, or pork.*

# Duck Confit on a Sweet Potato and Mushroom Hash with Mandarin Purée

**Confit of Duck**
**Ingredients**
4 duck legs
1 clove of garlic
1 bay leaf
1 sprig of thyme
4 tablespoons coarse sea salt
675ml to 900ml of duck fat rendered

**Method – Pre-heat oven to 150°c/fan oven130°c/gas 2**
Mix together garlic, bay leaf, thyme and course sea salt. Rub the seasoning into the duck legs and arrange them in one layer in a dish. Cover and refrigerate overnight.

Take out duck from the refrigerator. Under cold running water, rinse off the salt mixture, and pat dry. Arrange duck in one layer in a large saucepan. Melt the duck fat and pour over the duck legs, cover the pan with a layer of aluminium foil. Bake in the oven for three hours or until the meat is tender.

Place duck legs in an airtight container and cover with duck fat strained through a fine sieve. Refrigerate until ready to use.

**Sweet Potato and Mushroom Hash**
Grapeseed oil
¼ cup pine nuts
1lb assorted fresh mushrooms
2 shallots finely chopped
3 maris piper potato, cut into ½ inch cubes
4 Spring onions finely chopped
3 sweet potatoes cut into ½ inch cubes
½ large red onion finely chopped
2 cloves of garlic, finely chopped
(½ bunch of finely chopped coriander optional)
(2 tablespoons balsamic vinegar optional)

**To Prepare the Hash Pre-heat the Oven to 375f/gas 5/190c**
Spread the pine nuts on a baking sheet and toast for 5 minute until golden brown, set aside.

Put one tablespoon grapeseed oil in a large pan then add half of the mushrooms and sauté over a high heat for five minutes or until golden and all the liquid has evaporated. Transfer to a bowl and repeat the process with the remaining mushrooms, shallots and garlic to the pan and cook until they are translucent, season with salt and pepper. Set aside.

Bring two medium saucepans of salted boiling water to a boil and cook the maris pipers until just tender. Cook the sweet potato until tender, drain and transfer the potatoes to a large bowl.

Heat 2 tablespoons of grapeseed oil in a large pan, add the red onion and cook over a medium heat stirring for about five minutes. Add half the potatoes and cook for about five minutes or until tender and golden brown. Transfer the potatoes to a large bowl. Add the remaining oil to the pan and repeat the process, finally add the mushroom mixture to the potatoes adjust seasoning and keep warm

**Mandarin**
4 mandarins
Stock syrup (see page 128)

**Method**
Place the mandarins in a small saucepan, cover with water and bring to the boil. Strain the mandarins and cover with cold water and repeat the process another seven times, this removes the bitterness in the skin.

Once all the blanching has been done, cover the mandarins in stock syrup and simmer for two hours, take off the heat and allow the mandarins to cool, once cooled, place the mandarins and about 100ml if syrup into a liquidiser and blend to a smooth purée. Pass the purée through a fine sieve and store in the fridge.

**To Cook the Duck Confit**
Put two tablespoons of duck oil into a pan and allow to get hot, add the duck legs which have been drained from the cooking oil. Place in the pan and cook for 30 seconds, then place in the oven until crisp. Remove and keep warm.

**To Serve**
Spoon a pile of sweet potato and mushroom hash in the centre of 4 pre-heated dinner plates, pat the crispy duck confit leg on top and pat some of the mandarin purée around.

# Roasted Pork Tenderloin with Cider Pepper Glaze

**Pork**

**Ingredients – Serves 6**

2 trimmed pork tenderloins
210ml olive oil
2 teaspoon minced garlic
2 teaspoon minced rosemary
2 teaspoon minced fresh thyme
2 teaspoons minced sage

**Method**

Combine the olive oil, garlic, rosemary, thyme and sage in a tray.
Add the pork and turn to thoroughly coat cover and refrigerate over
night. Remove the meat from the marinade; pat dry with paper towels
and season to taste with salt place pork tenderloins in a hot frying
pan and cook until golden brown all over.

Place the pork tenderloins in a roasting tray and put in the oven.
Cook for four minutes then add some of the cider pepper glaze and
continue to cook for another six-eight minutes remove from the oven
and allow to rest for five minutes. Pour on a little more of the cider
glaze, carve the pork and place on four heated dinner plates, serve
with a potato of your choice and vegetables.

**Cider pepper glaze**

450ml unsweetened apple cider
1 large, peeled granny smith apple cut up into ½ inch pieces
2 tablespoons cider vinegar
2 tablespoons honey
1 teaspoon minced garlic
1 sprig of fresh thyme
1 teaspoon mustard seeds
3 juniper berries, crushed
1 teaspoon freshly ground pepper

**Method**

Combine the apple cider, apple, vinegar, honey, garlic, thyme,
mustard seeds and juniper berries in a medium stainless steel
saucepan and bring to a boil over a high heat. Lower the heat to
medium and simmer for 20minutes or until the apples are tender.
Strain the mixture into another saucepan; add the pepper and cook
over a high heat for 15 minutes to 20 minutes or until reduced to
110ml.

# Braised Beef Brisket with Balsamic Mushrooms and a Pumpkin Seed Crust

........................................................

## Ingredients – Serves 4-6
1kg.350/3lb piece beef brisket
Grapeseed oil
Mushrooms stalks (from the balsamic mushrooms for flavour)
4 sticks celery
1 onion roughly chopped
1 carrot roughly chopped
4 cloves garlic peeled
Thyme
Rosemary
300ml red wine
2 tablespoons chopped parsley

## Method
### Pre-heat oven to 170°c/fan oven 150°c/gas 3
In a casserole sear the beef on a high heat with the oil until well brown, drain excess oil then add the vegetables, garlic, herbs, salt and pepper. Deglaze with red wine and reduce by half. Cover with cold water and braise in the oven covered for three hours. Allow to cool in the stock. Remove the beef brisket and shred into long strands, taking care to remove any fat or gristle.

Chop up half of the balsamic mushrooms and add to the shredded beef with the chopped parsley and moisten with a few tablespoons of the reduced sauce, season with salt and pepper and press into stainless steels rings, refrigerate.

Slice one of the balsamic mushrooms and press on to the top and bottom of the rings, finally top with a good sprinkling of the pumpkin seed crust and place in the oven. Bake on a moderate 180°c/fan oven 160°c/gas 4 - oven for 8–10 minutes. Remove from the oven and allow to rest for a few minutes

## Roasted Balsamic Field Mushrooms (see page 90)
### Ingredients
6 x field mushrooms
50ml x balsamic vinegar
125ml x olive oil
6 x sprigs thyme

## Method
### Pre-heat the oven 180°c / 360°f / gas 4
Toss the mushrooms with the balsamic vinegar, olive oil, thyme, salt and pepper to taste.

Place on a baking sheet and roast for 6 to 8 minutes or until tender, pat dry with pepper towels, slice on the diagonal and keep warm.

## Pumpkin Seed Crust
2 tablespoons flat leaf parsley, coarsely chopped
2 tablespoons unsalted butter, melted
1 tablespoon olive oil
100g Japanese Panko crumbs
1 teaspoon thyme leaves, chopped finely
3 tablespoons toasted pumpkin seeds

### Pre-heat oven to 200°c/fan oven 180°c/gas 6
Dry toast the pumpkin seeds in a frying pan for few minutes. Mix together all the herb crust ingredients and season with salt and pepper and put in a processor for a few short blasts.

## The Sauce
Strain the stock into a saucepan and reduce until the right consistency, check seasoning and strain through a sieve. Port or Madeira can be added when you reduce the sauce to add more flavour.

## To Serve
Place the beef brisket on four pre-heated starter plates pour some of the reduced sauce around and serve, I like to serve this with roasted beetroots and red wine shallots (see page 134).

Poached Ballantine
of Rabbit on Warm
Lentil Salad and
Apple Aïoli

**Ingredients – Serves 6**

3lb x rabbit – boned and cut into ¼ inch dice
1x chicken breast boned
100g x boiled ham
85g x chicken livers
Salt and pepper to taste
1 x tablespoon Dijon mustard
1 x tablespoon of finely chopped parsley
1 x teaspoon finely chopped thyme
1 x medium egg
2 x slices of Parma ham

## Method

Mix all the ingredients together. Lay two slices of Parma ham on buttered silicone paper lined with aluminium foil and place the rabbit ingredients on to the ham and wrap the foil around into a sausage shape, about 4cm/1½ inches diameter. Poach in simmering water for fifteen minutes. Remove from the heat and allow to cool in water. Slice and serve hot or cold.

## Lentil Salad

225g green lentils
Sprig of thyme
½ bay leaf
Clove of garlic
15g butter
Brunoise – carrot, celery, leek and shallot (see page 136)

## Method

Put the lentils, thyme, bay leaf and garlic in a pan and add enough cold water to cover. Bring to the boil and simmer for 25 minutes. Drain the lentils; remove the herbs and garlic and leave to cool. To serve heat the butter in a frying pan over a moderate heat. Sweat the brunoise of vegetables until soft. Add the lentils and cook gently to warm through.

## Apple Aïoli

3 eggs yolks
1 clove of garlic
1 tablespoon Dijon mustard
1 tablespoon cider vinegar
100ml vegetable or light olive oil
200g apple purée
50ml apple juice
Salt and pepper

## Method

Put eggs yolks, garlic, mustard and vinegar into a food processor and with the motor running slowly add the oil. Finally add the apple juice and apple purée, season with salt and pepper and keep in the refrigerator until needed.

## To Serve

Place 1 tablespoon of puy lentils on the centre of a starter plate, slice the rabbit ballantine and place on top, put some apple aïoli on the plate around the rabbit and serve with lightly dressed salad leaves.

# Loin of Devonshire Lamb with Creamy Garlic and Rosemary Polenta and Pea Foam

......................................................................

### Ingredients – Serves 4
**For the lamb**
6 x 150g lamb loins, trimmed
Rapeseed oil
Salt and freshly ground black pepper

### Method
**Pre-heat oven to 230°c/gas 8**
Heat the oil in a frying pan and when hot add the lamb loins and seal on all sides, lift the lamb from the pan and put on a clean tray, cook in the oven for six minutes then remove the lamb from the pan and allow to rest in a warm place for five minutes.

### Creamy Garlic and Rosemary Polenta
1 tablespoon unsalted butter
1 tablespoon olive oil
1 teaspoon minced garlic
350ml double cream
350ml whole milk
350ml double cream

1/8 teaspoon cayenne pepper
½ teaspoon chopped rosemary
90g polenta (yellow cornmeal)
50g Parmesan cheese, freshly grated
Salt and pepper

### Method
In a large heavy bottom saucepan melt the butter over a medium heat. Add the oil and garlic, sweat the garlic for about 2 minutes but don't let it brown.

Add the cream, milk and water to the pan with the chopped rosemary and increase the heat to high. Add the cayenne pepper and let simmer for 5 minutes whisking constantly, pour the cornmeal into the boiling liquid in thin stream and cook stirring all the time with a wooden spoon until the polenta begins to thicken, stir in the cheese, keep warm until ready to serve.

### Green Pea Sauce
30g butter
2 shallots, finely sliced
1 clove of garlic, crushed
300ml chicken stock
300g frozen peas
100ml double cream

### Method
For the green pea sauce, melt butter in a medium sized saucepan, add chicken stock and bring to the boil. Add peas and bring back to the boil and cook for 2 minutes. Add the cream and check the seasoning and liquidise. Pass the sauce through a fine sieve and keep warm. Set aside.

### To Assemble
Pat the desired amount of polenta in the centre of 4 warm dinner plates. Cut the lamb loin into three equal pieces. Arrange the lamb on the polenta and surround with the sauce. Accompany with wilted spinach and a selection of seasonal vegetables.

# Vegetable Dishes

# Tangle of Tart Greens

**Ingredients**

½ head of a small Savoy cabbage
2 rashers of smoked bacon
½ red onion, thinly sliced
1 bunch watercress, coarse stems removed
1 bunch of baby spinach
1 tablespoon sugar
2-3 tablespoons balsamic vinegar/or red wine vinegar
Salt and freshly ground pepper to taste

**Method**

Core and coarsely shred the cabbage with a sharp knife.  In a large saucepan sauté the bacon over a medium heat.  Add the onion and cabbage and sauté until the cabbage begins to wilt.  Add the sugar and vinegar and cook until the cabbage is tender but still a little crisp.  Remove the saucepan from the heat, toss in the watercress and season to taste.  Serve warm.

# Red Cabbage

**Ingredients**

1 head of red cabbage
2 tablespoons of balsamic or red wine vinegar
1 onion, finely slice
225ml red wine
2 Granny Smiths, grated
2 tablespoon redcurrant jelly
Salt and pepper to taste
Grapeseed oil

**Method**

Remove and discard any outer damaged leaves, cut into quarters and cut away the hard cores, thinly slice the cabbage.

Put the grapeseed oil in a large pan, heat and add the cabbage and the onion and stir for 10 minutes until softened, add the grated apple and redcurrant jelly, cook for 10 minutes. Add the red wine and vinegar reduce the heat and slowly cook for 45 minutes stirring occasionally. The liquid should have evaporated.

Serve hot.

> ### *Chef's Tips*
> *If you add one grated potato 20 minutes before the cabbage is cooked this will absorb the juices and stop the red cabbage juice running all over the plate when you serve up.*
>
> *The red cabbage can also be put in a low oven (160°c / fan oven 140°/gas 3) and left for about 40 minutes to 1 hour.*

# Sweet and Sour Leeks

**Ingredients**

1kg leeks
2 cloves of garlic
1 tablespoon sugar
4 tablespoons olive oil
Juice of 1 lemon
1 tablespoon soy sauce (optional)

**Method**

Clean the leeks thoroughly. Cut off the tough green part. Cut the leeks into longish slices. Fry the crushed garlic and sugar in hot oil until the sugar caramelises slightly. Add the leeks and turn them a little over moderate heat. Sprinkle with lemon juice. Cover and stew gently over a low heat until tender. Serve hot or cold.

**To Assemble**

Place a small mound of the leeks in the middle of each plate and place a goat's cheese parcel on top. Spoon round the beetroot dressing and decorate each plate with the tomato garnish.

# Butternut Squash Mousse

## Ingredients
675g butternut squash
3 large eggs
Large egg yolks
150ml double cream
White pepper
40g unsalted butter, softened

## Method
### Pre-heat the oven to 250°f/120°c/gas ½
Peel and seed the squash and cut it into 1¾ cups of diced squash.
Place in a medium saucepan over a medium heat with water to
cover add salt to taste and bring to boil, lower the heat and simmer
for 15 minutes or until very tender and almost falling apart, drain well.
Place on a non-stick baking sheet in a pre-heated oven for 15
minutes until quite dry. Remove from the heat.

### Raise the temperature to 325°f/170°/gas 3
Mix the eggs, egg yolks and cream in a food processor fitted with a
metal blade until well blended. Add the squash and salt to taste and
process until very smooth. Taste and adjust seasoning with salt and
pepper.

Generously butter 170ml/6oz timbales or small soufflé dishes. Pour
equal portions of the squash mixture into the buttered moulds.

Place the filled timbales in a baking pan large enough to hold them
comfortably. Add hot water to come halfway. Place in a pre-heated
oven and bake for 25 minutes or until a knife inserted into the centre
comes out clean. Remove from the oven and water bath. Allow to set
on a wire rack for 2-3 minutes before removing the mould, turn out on
to a warm platter or plates.

# Potato Knish

## Ingredients – Serves 4-6
4 large potatoes pricked with a fork
4 tablespoons chopped chives
4 tablespoons fresh coriander
2 tablespoons olive oil
Salt and pepper
3 sheets filo pastry
115g clarified butter

## Method
### Pre-heat oven to - gas 5/375°f/190°c
Bake the potatoes for about an hour until tender. When cool enough
to handle, peel and place the flesh in a medium bowl. Add a little olive
oil and lightly crush the potatoes, allow to cool. Then add fresh herbs
season with salt and pepper and set aside.

Butter one sheet of filo pastry with the clarified butter then repeat
with the second one, place on top of one another, place the potato in
a long strip on the long side of the rectangle and roll up like a sausage
roll. Place in the fridge to firm up, when needed cut into four equal
portions and place in a hot oven until golden brown and crispy.

## Method

Dissolve the saffron in the chicken stock in a saucepan over a medium heat. Remove from the heat and set aside. Heat the olive oil in a large saucepan at a medium-high temperature. Sear the onions for 2-3 minutes being careful not to burn them. Stir in the rice and wine and let the wine evaporate. Lower the heat and add enough chicken stock to cover the rice. Stir until the rice absorbs the stock. Then add the remaining chicken stock all at once and cook for 15 to 20 minutes, or until the rice is cooked most of the way but is still firm. Stir occasionally while it is cooking. Remove from the heat and place the pan in a bowl of ice water until the rice is cool.

Form the rice into 6 balls and cut each one in half. Flatten each shape to make a 4-inch patty. Place a spoonful of cheese in the centre of one patty. Cover it with another patty and seal the edges carefully, keeping the cheese in the middle. Repeat until you have 6 cheese-filled rice cakes. Cover the cakes in a plastic wrap and refrigerate them for 1-6 hours.

Heat the olive oil in a large frying pan at a medium high heat, dust the cakes with flour on both sides and fry them until they are golden brown. Blot the cakes on a paper towel. Serve warm.

### Vegetable Relish

8 ripe plum tomatoes, seeded
1 whole cucumber, peeled and seeded
1 each of green, yellow, and red bell pepper
1 medium red onion
8-10 fresh basil leaves, chopped
115ml olive oil
1 tablespoon lemon juice
Salt
Freshly ground black pepper

### Method

Dice the tomatoes, cucumber, bell pepper and onion into ¼ inch pieces. Combine the vegetables with the basil, olive oil, lemon juice, salt and pepper in a bowl. Allow the relish to stand for 15 minutes but not to stand for more than 4 hours. Serve at room temperature.

# Saffron Risotto Cake with Cheese and Vegetable Relish

### Ingredients – Risotto Cakes

10 threads of saffron
950 ml chicken or vegetable stock
1 tablespoon olive oil
½ medium onion, finely chopped
550g Arborio rice
115ml dry white wine
225g mascarpone or cream cheese
115ml olive oil
Flour

# Gratin Dauphinois

**Ingredients – Serves 6**
4 medium-sized potatoes
75ml (3 fl oz) milk
75 ml (3 fl oz) double cream
Salt
Pinch of nutmeg
1 garlic clove
15 ml (1 tbsp) clarified butter

**Method**
Peel the potatoes and slice very finely on a mandolin.  Soak in cold water to remove the starch. Boil together the milk and the cream, season with salt and add the nutmeg. Rub a 15 x 30.5 cm (6 x 12 inch) rectangular roasting pan with garlic.  Brush it with clarified butter.

Drain the potatoes and dry thoroughly on absorbent kitchen paper.  Spread the potatoes in thin, closely-packed layers, adding a little creamy liquid between each layer.

The mixture should not be more than 2cm (¾ inch) thick.  Pour the rest of the liquid on top and bake in the oven at 180c (350f) mark 4 for about 30-45 minutes or until nicely browned on top.

**Potato and Apple Gratin**
150g green apples
300g potatoes
100g onions
130g butter
1 clove of garlic, peeled
Salt and pepper
200 ml cream
80g grated tasty cheese

**Method**
**Pre-heat the oven to 180°c/fan oven 160°c/gas 4**
Peel the apples and grate them into a bowl, peel the potatoes and cut them in thin slices, peel and slice the onions and sweat them together with the apples in 100g butter.  Allow to cool and mix them with the sliced potatoes.

Chop the garlic and add it together with the salt and pepper.  Butter a gratin dish, put in the mixture and pour the cream equally over the mix and sprinkle with cheese.  Place the dish in the oven on the bottom shelf for approximately 1 hour.

Use a pastry cutter to cut out the portions you require, when cold and re-heat in the oven.  The potato gratin will keep for 5 days covered in the fridge.

# Red Wine Shallots

## Ingredients

4 shallots, finely chopped
2 cloves garlic, finely chopped
2 tomatoes, peeled, seeded and diced
30ml olive oil
175ml red wine
Few sprigs rosemary
500ml lamb jus

## Method

Sauté shallots, garlic and tomatoes in olive oil, de-glaze with red wine and reduce by half the volume. Add rosemary and lamb stock, reduce to required consistency and pass through a fine sieve. Season and serve.

# Wild Mushroom Salsa

## Ingredients

225g x shitake mushrooms
1 x teaspoon salt
225g x English mushrooms
1 x teaspoon pepper
225g x chanterelle mushrooms
3 x tablespoons olive oil
3 x tablespoons chopped chives or spring onions
2 x tablespoons chopped fresh coriander
3 x tablespoons chopped black olives
Lime juice to taste

## Method

Clean each of the mushrooms and cut them in a small even dice, warm the olive oil in a sauté pan when hot sauté the mushrooms quickly. Season with salt and pepper and allow the mixture to cool. Add the remaining ingredients to the mushroom mix and combine well.

# Spicy Fruit Relish

### Ingredients

1 teaspoon olive oil
115g red pepper, cored, seeded and chopped
1 green pepper, cored, seeded and chopped
½ large onion, chopped
50g brown sugar + 2 x teaspoons
¼ teaspoon salt
1 large clove garlic, finely chopped
85g currants
¼ teaspoon turmeric
¼ teaspoon dried mustard
¼ teaspoon cayenne pepper
1 tablespoon fresh ginger, peeled and chopped finely
3 medium apples, cored and chopped
3 large pears, cored and chopped (225g)
170ml white wine vinegar

### Method

In a large stainless steel saucepan, heat the olive oil. Stir in the red and green pepper, onion, 2 x teaspoons of brown sugar, ginger and garlic over a medium heat, stirring occasionally until the vegetables are wilted, 6-8 minutes.

Stir in the currants and the remaining brown sugar, mustard, cayenne, turmeric, salt, and vinegar. Continue to cook for 10 minutes longer. Add the apples and cook for 2 x minutes then add the pears, cook until the fruit is tender (the firmer fruit is added first)

Correct seasoning to taste and cool, transfer to one or two containers and refrigerate, covered until needed.

# Cranberry Relish

### Ingredients

Zest and juice 1 medium orange
225ml red wine
350 g fresh cranberries
½ medium onion, diced
25g fresh root ginger, peeled and cut into julienne strips
3 tablespoons of dark brown sugar
4 cm piece of cinnamon stick
2 tablespoons Grand Marnier

### Method

Cut the orange into julienne strips. Heat the juices in a small saucepan with a quarter of the wine and cook until tender, about 10 minutes.

In a medium saucepan, combine the cranberries, onion and the rest of the wine, ginger, brown sugar, salt and pepper with the cinnamon and cook until the relish thickens, approximately 15-20 minutes, stirring occasionally.

Stir in the Grand Marnier and the reserved orange mixture and remove the piece of cinnamon. Cool and transfer to a serving bowl. Refrigerate until needed.

# Creamy Garlic and Rosemary Polenta

**Ingredients**

1 tablespoon unsalted butter
1 tablespoon olive oil
1 teaspoon minced garlic
350ml double cream
350ml whole milk
350ml double cream

1/8 teaspoon cayenne pepper
½ teaspoon chopped rosemary
90g polenta (yellow cornmeal)
50g Parmesan cheese, freshly grated
Salt and pepper

**Method**

In a large heavy bottom saucepan melt the butter over a medium heat. Add the oil and garlic, sweat the garlic for about 2 minutes but don't let it brown.

Add the cream, milk and water to the pan with the chopped rosemary and increase the heat to high. Add the cayenne pepper and let simmer for 5 minutes whisking constantly, pour the cornmeal into the boiling liquid in thin stream and cook stirring all the time with a wooden spoon until the polenta begins to thicken, stir in the cheese, keep warm until ready to serve.

# Lightly Spiced Aubergine

**Ingredients**

900g x fresh aubergines
2 x tablespoons sun-dried tomatoes
5 x tablespoons olive oil
1 x small onion and finely diced about 50g
2 x finely diced cloves of garlic
1 x tablespoon ground cumin
50g x coriander
1 x packet of filo pastry
50g x unsalted butter

**Method**

Cut the aubergines in half lengthwise, brush with olive oil, lie on a baking sheet and roast for 30 minutes, remove from the oven and cool. When cool, scoop the pulp away from the skin, discard the skin, heat the olive oil in a large frying pan and sauté the onions until translucent. Add the garlic and continue to cook for one minute more. Do not allow the garlic to brown, add the cumin, salt and pepper, mix well and set aside to cool.

# Wild Rice Pancakes

**Makes about 15 pancakes**
1 tablespoon chopped spring onions
2 teaspoon grapeseed oil
1 teaspoon butter
1 egg
1 egg yolk
1 teaspoon of cumin
225ml milk
225g plain flour
1 tablespoon baking powder
350g cooked wild rice
1 tablespoon of fresh herbs, optional
Oil for cooking

**Wild Rice Pancakes**
Sauté the spring onions in grapeseed oil for 2 minutes, place the egg, egg yolk and milk in a medium bowl and whisk until well blended.  Sift together the flour and baking powder add the egg mixture and whisk until smooth.  Fold in the wild rice, herbs etc.

**Cooking the Pancakes**
Heat two tablespoons of grapeseed oil in a pan and place one good heaped tablespoon of wild rice pancake mixture into the oil to form a 5cms/2-inch pancake.  Repeat four times.  Cook for one minute then flip over and cook on the other side for two minutes more.  Remove from the pan and set aside and keep warm.

# Butternut Squash Purée

**Makes 500ml**
1 onion, finely sliced
Grapeseed oil
500g chopped butternut squash
3 tablespoons butter, unsalted
Salt and pepper to taste

**Pre-heat the oven to 200°c/fan oven 180°c/gas 6**
Sauté the onions in a little grapeseed oil without colouring them until soft.  Place in a small roasting tray with remaining ingredients, add a splash of water.  Cover the tray with tinfoil and pierce a few holes to let the steam to escape, place in the oven until the butternut squash is soft.

Place the butternut squash in a food processor and process to a smooth puree with the unsalted butter, check the seasoning and keep warm.

# Caponata

**Ingredients**

3 x medium aubergines
6 x celery sticks, peeled and cut on the diagonal into 2cm pieces
2 x red peppers, sliced
2 x red onions cut into thin wedges
Extra olive oil
1 x level dessertspoon capers
1.5kg tomatoes, quartered
3 x garlic cloves, chopped
100ml x red wine vinegar
30g castor sugar
Salt and black pepper
A few basil leaves
Toasted pinenuts (optional)

**Method**

**Pre-heat oven 160°c/fan oven 140°c/gas 3**
Cut the aubergines into chunks of about 3cm. Heat a frying pan with oil and fry the pieces in two batches until golden brown. Remove from the oil and set aside.

In the same pan sweat the peppers, celery, onion and capers in the olive oil, with a good pinch of salt and pepper, after 10 minutes when everything is soft remove from the pan and place in a roasting tin with the cooked aubergine. Scatter over the tomatoes and chopped garlic and pour over the red wine vinegar. Add the sugar, salt and pepper.

Put in the oven for about one hour, give a big stir and serve warm or at room temperature (never hot) with torn basil leaves and toasted pinenuts (if used) folded through.

# Deep-fried Cauliflower with Garlic and Paprika Oil

**Ingredients**

450g cauliflower floret
2 tablespoons of olive oil
2 cloves of garlic, crushed
2 tablespoons white wine vinegar
1 tablespoon paprika
3 tablespoons hot water
Sunflower oil for deep-frying
Salt and pepper

**Batter**

75g plain flour
5 teaspoons cornflour
Pinch if salt
2 teaspoons baking powder
175ml water

**Method**

To make the batter mix all the ingredients together in a bowl until smooth. Cover and chill until needed. Bring a pan of water to the boil and cook the cauliflower for 5-6 minutes until almost tender, drain and leave to cool.

To make garlic and paprika oil, heat the olive oil in a frying pan over a medium heat. Add the garlic and cook gently for one minute to flavour the oil then remove with a slotted spoon. Pour vinegar into the oil and add paprika and water and cook stirring continuously for one minute. Set aside.

Heat the sunflower oil in a small heavy based pan. Dip the cauliflower into the batter and deep fry for 2-3 minutes. Remove with a slotted spoon and drain on kitchen paper. Transfer to a serving dish and pour the paprika oil over to serve.

# Herb Vinaigrette

50ml balsamic vinegar
3 tablespoons Dijon mustard
2 tablespoons flat leaf parsley
2 tablespoons basil
2 tablespoons chives
225ml olive oil
Salt and freshly ground pepper

### Method

Combine the vinegar and mustard in the bowl of a food processor, add the herbs with the processor running then add the olive oil very slowly until the mixture emulsifies. The dressing will keep for 7 days covered in the fridge.

### Basil or Chive Oil

15g fresh basil leaves
225ml olive oil
1 teaspoon salt

### Method

Blanch the basil leaves in salted boiling water for 30 seconds, cool the basil leaves in iced water then dry and drain on paper towels.  Place the basil leaves and oil in a blender and purée then strain the oil and refrigerate.  Keeps for 1 to 2 days.

### Curry Oil

Ingredients
60g chopped onion
170ml oil
1 apple peeled cored and diced roughly
2 tablespoons curry powder

### Method

Sauté the onion and apple in 2 tablespoons of oil for 5 minutes.  Add the curry powder and cook for 3 minutes.  Purée the mixture with the remaining oil.  Refrigerate for 1 day then strain through a fine mesh sieve.  Let it stand for 3 hours then carefully decant.

# Balsamic Glaze

6 oranges freshly squeezed
1 small bottle of balsamic vinegar

In a saucepan combine the orange juice and balsamic vinegar and reduce until mixture turns syrupy.  Strain through a fine sieve into a jar.  Cool and cover.  Keep refrigerated for up to 6 weeks.

# Asian Coleslaw

### Ingredients

300g shredded green cabbage
50g julienne of carrots
1 onion, finely chopped
Salt and freshly ground black pepper
1 cup cider vinegar
2 cloves
3 shallots, chopped
10 black peppercorns
1 jalapeño pepper, sliced
3 ¼ inch slices of peeled ginger
225ml cup olive oil

### Method

Combine the cabbage, carrots and onion in a large bowl and season lightly with salt and pepper.

Combine the vinegar, garlic, shallots, peppercorns, jalapeño and ginger in a saucepan and simmer for 5 minutes.  Remove from the heat and cool.  Strain through a fine-mesh sieve and whisk in the olive oil.  Pour the liquid over the cabbage mixture and toss well.  Season to taste with salt and pepper.

# Herb Crêpes with Sweet Potato, Goat's Cheese and a Tomato Saffron Sauce

. . . . . . . . . . . . . . . . . . . . . . . . . . . . . . . . . . . . . . . . .

**Crêpes**
**Ingredients – Serves 4**
150g plain flour
1 egg
180ml milk
2 tablespoons grapeseed oil
1 tablespoon finely chopped chives
½ tablespoon finely chopped chervil
½ tablespoon finely chopped basil

**Method**
Sift flour into a large bowl. Combine egg, milk, and grapeseed oil, 90ml water and ¼ teaspoon salt in a separate bowl and whisk well. Make a well in the centre of the flour and slowly add the liquid, whisking until combined, stir through the herbs, transfer to a jug and stand for 30 minutes.

Heat 1 teaspoon of butter in a crêpe pan over a medium heat, then pour enough batter to just cover the base of the pan, (pour excess back into jug). Cook crêpes for 1 minute each side, transfer to a plate, and repeat with remaining mixture.

**Sweet Potato and Goat's Cheese Filling**
**Ingredients**
600g sweet potato, peeled and cut into 2cm pieces
60ml extra virgin olive oil

150g soft goat's cheese, crumbled
55g toasted pine nuts

**Method**
**Pre-heat oven to 190°c if using a fan oven, follow manufactures instructions/gas 5/375°f**
Place the sweet potato on a roasting tray and drizzle with olive oil and season with sea salt. Roast for 25 minutes or until soft. Cool. Combine the goat's cheese and season to taste.

Divide sweet potato mixture between 2 crêpes and roll each into a log and wrap tightly in cling film. Refrigerate for 1 hour, remove and cut each into 3 pieces in an upright position on a baking tray, sprinkle with parmesan cheese.

**Reduce oven - 180°c / fan oven 160°c/ gas 4** When you have the balsamic mushrooms (see page 90) and sauce ready bake crêpes for 10 minutes or until just golden.

**Saffron tomato sauce**
115g red onion, sliced finely
2 tablespoons vegetable oil
200g peeled seeded and chopped tomatoes
1 tablespoon balsamic vinegar
55g chopped sun dried tomatoes
A pinch of saffron threads
125ml passata

**Method**
Cook the red onions in the vegetable oil over a medium heat for 2 – minutes or until caramelised. Add the tomatoes, passata, sun dried tomatoes and balsamic vinegar. Cook for 10 minutes then add saffron and cook for 2 minutes more stirring occasionally. Remove from the heat, this sauce can be served as it is but for a finer sauce purée until smooth and pass through a sieve. Season with salt and pepper and keep warm.

**Presentation***
Remove crêpes from the oven, place the balsamic mushrooms then the pancakes on four pre-heated dinner plates, sprinkle with Parmesan cheese and pour the saffron tomato sauce around, serve immediately.

# Coconut Rice

**Ingredients**
225g Basmati rice, rinsed
2 tablespoons olive oil
½ onion, diced
½ clove garlic, finely chopped
knob grated ginger
½ teaspoon turmeric
600ml water
115g coconut cream
½ lemon, juice of
Seasoning

**Method**
Sweat the onion and garlic in the olive oil until tender. Add the rice and turmeric, stir so that the oil and turmeric coat the rice then add the liquid with the coconut cream and stir well.

Put a lid on and place in a cool oven for 20 minutes.

After this, bring out and fork through adding some lemon juice and check for seasoning.

# Asian Vegetables with a Hot Sauce

**Ingredients**
1 small onion, coarsely chopped
2 cloves garlic
10 peppercorns
1 teaspoon dried shrimps pounded
3 birds eye chilli's to taste
Juice of 2 limes (or 1 lemon)
1 teaspoon palm or (brown) sugar
2 teaspoons shrimp paste
Coconut milk

**Method**
Mix the onion, garlic and peppercorns in a food processor to a coarse paste. Add the dried shrimps and chilli's, continue mixing and finally add the gapi (shrimp paste). Adjust the seasoning if needed, it should be slightly sharp and very hot. Cook the vegetables in coconut milk and serve the hot paste in a small bowl.

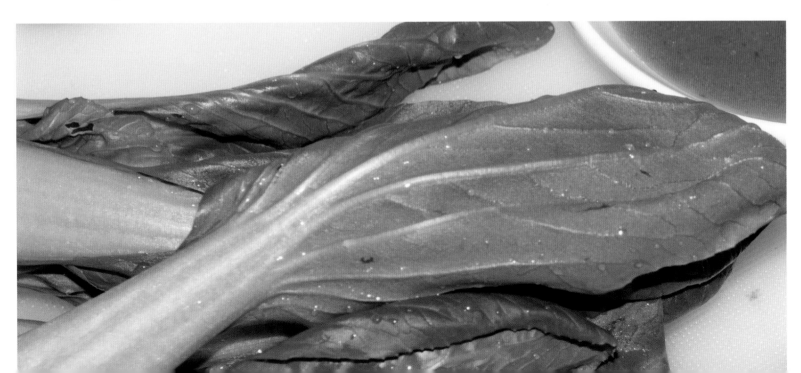

# Roasted Balsamic Field Mushrooms

**Serves 6**
Balsamic mushrooms taste good in a salad or used as a stuffing for chicken breast

**Ingredients**
6 field mushrooms
50ml balsamic vinegar
125ml olive oil
6 sprigs thyme
2 cloves garlic, finely sliced

**Method**
**Pre-heat oven to180°c – if using a fan oven follow manufactures instructions / gas 4/350°f**
Toss the mushrooms with the balsamic vinegar, olive oil, thyme, garlic, salt, and pepper to taste.  Place on a baking sheet and roast for 6 to 8 minutes or until tender, pat dry with pepper towels, slice on the diagonal and keep warm.

90

# Gratin of Courgettes

**Ingredients**
55g butter
1kg courgettes, sliced
2 cloves garlic, crushed
140ml double cream
5 egg yolks
Salt and freshly ground pepper
55g parmesan cheese or cheddar

**Method**
**Pre-heat the oven to 180°c/fan oven 160°c/gas 4**
Melt the butter in a saucepan and cook the courgettes.  Mash well with a potato masher, then place in a clean tea towel and squeeze out as much water as possible (to form a firm purée).  Put the courgettes in a bowl and stir in the eggs.  Season to taste and pour into a gratin dish and sprinkle over the cheese and bake in the oven for about 20 minutes until golden brown.

# Maple Glazed Root Vegetables

**Serves 4-6**
This is a cosy winter accompaniment to roasted poultry and game.

**Ingredients**
4 tablespoons unsalted butter
2 onions, diced
3 leeks, split in half and chopped
6 carrots peeled and sliced into ¼ inch rounds
1 large turnip peeled and diced (optional)
3–4 parsnips, peeled and cut into ¼ inch rounds
125ml maple syrup
225ml chicken stock
salt and freshly ground pepper to taste
1 tablespoon crushed cardamom seeds

**Method**
Heat 1 tablespoon butter in a large frying pan until it begins to brown. Add the onions and leeks and sauté for 10 minutes until they begin to caramelise. Remove from the heat and allow to cool. Combine the remaining ingredients except the butter in an ovenproof casserole dish, dot the top with the remaining butter cover with aluminium foil and bake for 45 minutes. Uncover and continue to cook for another 15 minutes until well glazed.

# Quince Purée

**Ingredients**
1kg very ripe quinces – or pears or apples
2litres cold water – acidulated with 2 tablespoons of vinegar
Juice of 1 lemon
100g castor sugar
40g  unsalted butter

**Method**
Peel, core and quarter the quinces and cut roughly into 2.5cm/1- inch squares, dropping them into a bowl with 2 litres of acidulated water as you go. In a large saucepan, bring to the boil 500ml of cold water with the lemon juice and sugar.

Drain quinces and put them in the boiling water, cover and simmer for 15 minutes or until soft. Drain in a colander then purée into a medium saucepan and stir until completely smooth.

Pour the purée into a medium saucepan and stir until the desired consistency is reached. Add a pinch of your favourite spice and set aside to keep warm.

# Baked Goat's Cheese in Indian Pastry with Sweet & Sour Leeks

**Ingredients – Serves 4**
**Indian Pastry**
225g x plain flour
1 x egg
2 x tablespoons olive oil
1 x teaspoon curry powder
Pinch of salt
100ml x yoghurt
1 x tablespoon water
1 x teaspoon cumin

**Goat's Cheese in Indian Pastry**
55g x roughly chopped hazelnuts, chestnuts and pistachios
175g x goat's cheese
55g x butter

**Sweet and Sour Leeks**
2 x large leeks
1x tablespoon sugar
Juice of 1 x lemon
2 x cloves of garlic
4 x tablespoons olive oil
1 x tablespoon soy sauce (optional)

**Indian Pastry – Method**
In a mixing bowl combine the flours with the spice mix, cumin and curry powder. Make a well in the middle and add the salt, egg, yoghurt, oil and water and mix to a smooth dough. Knead for 5 minutes and then allow to rest for 30 minutes. If the pastry feels a little wet just add some more flour.

> *Chef's Tip*
> *Indian Pastry is very versatile and can be pan-fried lightly or baked in the oven.*

**Goat's Cheese in Indian pastry – Method**
**Pre-heat oven to 200°C/fan oven 180°C/gas 6**
Cut the goat's cheese into the desired shape for wrapping in the pastry and place on a flat surface and brush with butter and sprinkle over the chopped nuts and then set aside. Roll out the Indian pastry and cut four round circles large enough for the cheese and shape the pastry around the cheese and tuck the ends underneath. Repeat with the others. Place in the fridge to firm for five minutes.

Heat up a frying pan with a little oil and cook the goat's cheese parcels until golden brown, be careful they do not burn. Place on an oven tray and set aside. (These parcels can also be deep-fried until golden brown and puffed up).

**Sweet and Sour Leeks – Method**
Clean the leeks thoroughly. Cut off the tough green part. Cut the leeks into longish slices. Fry the crushed garlic and sugar in hot oil until the sugar caramelises slightly. Add the leeks and turn them a little over moderate heat. Sprinkle with lemon juice. Cover and stew gently over a low heat until tender. Serve hot or cold.

**Assembly**
Return the goat's cheese to the oven for four minutes or until hot. Place a small mound of the leeks in the middle of each plate and place a goat's cheese parcel on top. This dish will be good with a tomato dressing or red pepper and basil.

**Chef's Tip**
*You can use a pasta machine to roll out the pastry very thin just like pasta lasagne sheets if you like.*

# Pea Pancakes

**Ingredients**
225g fresh or frozen peas, cooked and well drained
1 medium egg, plus 1 egg yolk
125ml double cream
4 tablespoons plain flour
25g butter
Seasoning

**Method**
Blend all the ingredients, except the butter, in a processor until smooth. Heat the butter in a frying pan, spoon in batter to make a 7.5cm round and cook for 2 minutes until set. Turn and cook the other side for 2 minutes until golden. Drain and keep hot. Repeat to make eight pancakes.

# Sweet Pepper Ragout

**Ingredients – Serves 4**
1 red and 1 yellow, cored, seeded and diced
50ml olive oil
1 onion chopped finely
4 cloves of garlic, crushed and chopped finely
Pinch of cayenne pepper
1 tablespoon fresh herbs, parsley and basil
225ml passata
125ml dry white wine
Salt and freshly ground white pepper

**Method**
In heavy sauce pan, heat 50ml of olive oil, sauté the onion, onion, garlic and cayenne pepper together for 5 minutes. Stir in the tomatoes, peppers and saffron.

Pour in the white wine and reduce by half over a medium heat until all the liquid is absorbed. Add the passata and cook for 15 minutes, season and add the fresh herbs. Keep warm.

# Goat's Cheese and Artichoke Spring Rolls with Rocket and a Tomato Salad

**Spring Rolls – Serves 4**
175g fresh Goats cheese without a rind
75g cold mashed potato
25g freshly grated Parmesan cheese
1 coarsely chopped globe artichoke
½ teaspoon cornflour
1 egg white
8 spring roll wrappers (6 inches square)

**Rocket and Tomato Salad**
150g loosely packed rocket lettuce
200g ½ inch diced peeled tomato
1 tablespoon thinly sliced red onions

**Garnish**
Kalamata olives
Freshly grated Parmesan cheese
Blanched fresh beans

**Spring Roll Filling**
Mix all the spring roll ingredients together and check seasoning, set aside.

**To Assemble the Spring Rolls**
In a small bowl whisk together the cornflour and egg white to make an egg wash.

Divide the filling into 8 cylinders, each 1 inch by 3 inches long. Lay out a wrapper in a diamond shape on a work surface, place a goat's cheese cylinder horizontally on the bottom third of the wrapper.

Bring the bottom point over the goat's cheese and tuck the point underneath it. Begin rolling tightly until you reach the side points then fold the sides in at a neat angle, continue rolling until there is a triangle of about 2 inches from the top. Brush the edges of the wrapper with egg wash and complete rolling. Transfer to a baking sheet and cover with a towel and refrigerate, repeat with the remaining wrappers.

**To Deep-fry the Spring Rolls**
Heat 3 inches of oil in a deep, heavy pot or fryer to 360°. Deep-fry the spring rolls 2 at a time until golden brown, about 3-4 minutes, using tongs transfer the spring rolls to paper towels to drain, keep warm in a warm oven.

**Salad**
In a bowl toss the salad ingredients with a vinaigrette dressing, divide the salad among 4 plates, top each plate with 2 spring rolls. Arrange the olives around the spring rolls and sprinkle with parmesan cheese.

**Tomato Oil**
225ml fresh tomato juice
225ml olive oil or grape seed oil

**To Prepare the Tomato Oil**
Cook the tomato juice over heat for 20 minutes, or until reduced by half. Strain through a fine mesh sieve and let cool to room temperature. When cool, whisk in the olive oil and season to taste with salt and pepper.

# Vegetable Tart with a Tomato, Ginger and Lemongrass Flavoured Sauce

**Ingredients**
Homemade or 1 x packet of shortcrust pastry
A selection of seasonal vegetables
500g x butternut squash, peeled and cut into small dice
250g baby beetroots washed and halved and root removed
2tsp x olive oil
Broccoli florets (blanch in boiling water and re-fresh in cold water, set aside and refrigerate)
Cauliflower florets          "          "          "
Fresh garden peas
120g c soft cream cheese
2 x eggs
1 x clove garlic, crushed
Salt and pepper to taste
1 x tablespoon of mixed fresh herbs, chives, basil etc

**Method**
**Pre-heat the oven – 200c/fan oven 180.c/gas 6**
Place the squash and beetroot on to a baking tray with the oil and toss to coat. Bake in the oven until beginning to colour.

Divide the pastry into six equal portions and roll out to 14cm rounds, press into lightly oiled 12cm round individual tartlet tins, prick the bases with a fork and bake for eight to ten minutes until just beginning to colour.

Whisk together the soft cream cheese, milk, eggs and herbs. Season to taste, place the vegetable evenly in the tartlet cases and bake for twelve to fifteen minutes until the filling is set.

**Ingredients**
**Tomato, Ginger and Lemon Grass Sauce**
40 x olive oil
10g x garlic finely chopped
40g x red onion, finely chopped
5g x finely chopped ginger
5g x finely chopped lemon grass
6 x large plum tomatoes, skinned and diced
10ml x fish sauce
5ml x lime juice
A pinch of salt and pepper

**Method**
Heat the oil and sauté the garlic, onion, ginger and lemon grass until soft. Add the tomatoes, fish sauce, lime juice and sugar. Simmer for ten minutes, season to taste. Add the chopped coriander leaves just before serving.

**Assembly**
Place a good spoonful of the tomato and ginger, lemon grass flavoured sauce on the centre of a dinner plate then place the tart on top and serve.

# Vegetable Strudel with Black Pepper and Tomato Chickpeas

**Ingredients – Serves 6**

3 tablespoons olive oil

225g peeled, seeded and diced tomato

225g onion   (julienne)

15g chopped green olives

225g mushrooms

salt and pepper to taste

225g  leeks

9 sheets filo pastry

225g carrots

2 sheets of mixed spices to your taste

½ tablespoon chopped garlic

## Method

Warm 2 x tablespoons of olive oil and sauté the onion until they are translucent.  Add the carrots, leeks and mushrooms and cook for 2 minutes.  Add the garlic then the tomato and olives, sauté for a minute and season with salt and pepper, remove from the heat and cool.

## To Make the Strudel

Pre-heat the oven to 400°.  Layer 3 x sheets of filo pastry brushing oil between each layer. (make sure to keep the rest of the filo sheets covered with a damp towel)  Cut the stacked sheets in half crosswise, spread about 3 x tablespoons of filling in each half sheet then roll it up like a wide cigar and cover.

When all the strudels are finished bake them on a baking sheet for 10 minutes until golden brown.

**Black Pepper and Tomato Chickpeas – Serves 6**

450g x dry chick peas

900ml x cold water

1 x bay leaf

1 x sprig of thyme

1 x tablespoon black pepper freshly ground

Salt to taste

2 x tablespoons chopped fresh parsley or 2 tablespoons pesto sauce

225ml x tomato passata

1 x medium lime, juiced

## Method

To cook the chickpeas – rinse the chickpeas under cold running water, place them in a pot with the cold water add the bay leaf and a little salt, simmer for 20 minutes then add the tomato passata and cook for a further 30 minutes.  Chickpeas should be cooked but still with firm centres, strain the chickpeas and set aside.  Add the bayleaf and thyme to the tomato mix, reduce to a sauce consistency.

Place the chickpeas in a bowl and season with the olive oil, chopped parsley and salt and pepper, mix well and cover the bowl with cling film.  After 5 minutes uncover and toss gently with a squeeze of fresh lime juice and the tomato sauce.

**To serve** – Split each strudel in half on a bias, serve with the hot black peppered chickpeas.

# Shallot and Balsamic Dressing

**Ingredients**
6 x large shallots
225ml x olive oil
3 x tablespoons balsamic vinegar
2 x tablespoons chopped fresh chives
Salt and pepper

**Method**
Prepare the vinaigrette - place the shallots and 175ml olive oil in a small ovenproof pan and cover tightly. Bake at 350°f/180°c/ fan oven 160°c/gas 4 for one hour, or until the shallots are soft. Let the shallots cool in the olive oil and then remove reserving the oil. Julienne the shallots and put them in a bowl, added the balsamic vinegar and slowly whisk in the reserved olive oil. Add the chopped chives and season to taste with salt and pepper.

**To Assemble**
Slice beef and place on pre-heated dinner plates, spoon some roasted shallots and balsamic vinaigrette on top. Serve with vegetables and potato of your choice.

# Warm Couscous Salad

**Ingredients – serves 4**
200g x couscous
2 x tablespoons raisins
1 x salt
15ml x olive oil
425ml x boiling water
1 x Granny Smith apple
20ml x lemon juice
5ml x finely grated lemon rind
1 x tablespoon finely chopped coriander

**Method**
Put the raisins into a small bowl, pour on a little boiling water to cover, and let soak for 10 minutes until softened and plumped up. Drain well and pat dry.

Put the couscous, salt, olive oil in a large bowl and pour over the 400ml boiling water. Give the mixture a quick stir, then cover with cling film and let soak for 15 to 20 minutes.

Peel, core and finely dice the apple then squeeze over a little lemon juice to prevent it from discolouring. Fork through the couscous to separate the grains and break up any large lumps. Add the apples together with the rest of the ingredients and fork through to mix. Taste and adjust the seasoning.

# Desserts

# Caramelised Maple Creams with Ginger Poached Pears and Almond Tuiles

........................................................

**Ingredients – Serves 8 using 125ml pudding moulds**
300g castor sugar
100ml water
500ml double cream
100ml milk
125ml pure maple syrup
2 eggs
4 egg yolks

**Method – Pre-heat oven to 150°c/300°f/gas 2**
Make a caramel by boiling the castor sugar and water over a moderate heat; pour the hot caramel into 6 x 150ml dariole moulds. Working quickly as the caramel will continue to cook and darken, tilt the moulds to ensure each is evenly lined with caramel then discard any excess and allow the caramel to cool.

Bring the cream, milk and maple syrup to simmering point in a saucepan over a medium heat. In a bowl whisk the eggs and egg yolks then slowly pour in the hot cream. Pour the egg and cream mixture through a fine meshed sieve over a jug, pour into the prepared moulds. Bake the creams in a water bath for 45 minutes or until just set. Remove the water bath from the oven and allow the creams to cool in it.

Remove the creams from the water and refrigerate them on a tray covered in cling film for 3 hours before serving.

**Poached Pears**
750ml sugar syrup (see page 128)
1 tablespoon minced fresh ginger

250ml Poire William liqueur
6 ripe pears

**Method**
Put the sugar syrup, fresh ginger, Poire William liqueur in a stainless steel saucepan and bring to a boil, simmer for 15 minute to intensify the flavour and reduce the liquid slightly. Peel, halve and core the pears and lay them gently in the poaching liquid. Press baking paper down ('cartouche' – see Chef's Tips below) on to the pears to keep submerged to ensure even cooking. Simmer gently until cooked and softened, about 30 minutes. Remove the pears from the poaching liquid then slice them in half again and set aside. Reduce liquid over medium heat until it reaches a syrupy consistency, set aside.

**Almond Tuile (see page 131)**

**To Serve**
Carefully turn out the maple creams on to the centre of each plate. Arrange 4 pear quarters around each cream and pour a little of the Poire William syrup over each pear. Top with the tuile and serve with an ice-cream of your choice.

**Chef's Tips**
**Maple Syrup** is syrup usually made from xylem sap or sugar maple, red maple or black maple trees. Maple syrup contains fewer calories and has a higher concentration of minerals than honey.

**Cartouche** – Is a circle of wax (greaseproof) paper that covers a dish during cooking preventing evaporation of liquid while allowing heat to escape.

# Lime Fromage Blanc Mousse with Lime and Tropical Fruit Compôte and Orange & Sesame Biscuits

**Ingredients – Serves 6 – 8**
70g castor sugar
175g cream cheese
45ml water
20ml stock syrup (see page 128)
2 egg yolks
500ml whipping cream, softly whipped
2 limes, grated zest
3 ½ leaves of gelatine

## Method
Put the gelatine in a cup of cold water to soak. In a bowl combine the castor sugar, 2 egg yolks, water, stock syrup and lime juice, cook in a Bain Marie or large basin over a saucepan of hot water whisking until the mixture has doubled in size.

Drain off the gelatine and whisk into the warm mixture, allow to cool slightly and whisk in the cream cheese and lime zest, continue to whisk until the mixture is smooth.

Transfer the mixture to a suitable sized tin lined with a double layer of cling film set in the fridge for 1-2 hours or until firm.

Slice into portion sizes.

## Lime and Tropical Fruit Compote
5 limes, zested and segmented, zest reserved
1 ripe mango
200g castor sugar
a few slices of fresh pineapple
200ml water
2 kiwis
50ml lime juice
All the fruit diced into concassé pieces
Fresh pomegranate (optional to decorate)

## Method
Boil the lime zest for 5 minutes. Strain and run under cold water, repeat this three times. Place the castor sugar in a dry pan and cook over moderate heat stirring until a light golden brown colour.

Add lime juice and water, reduce over gentle heat by three-quarters stirring occasionally allow to cool. Add the lime segments, zest and mango, pineapple, kiwi and allow to cool.

## To serve
Place a Fromage Blanc in the centre of a dessert plate, drizzle with lime and tropical fruit compote and finish with a sorbet of your choice.

## Orange & Sesame Biscuits
125ml orange juice
250g icing sugar
2 oranges, zested
90g plain flour
125g sesame seeds
90g butter, melted and warm

## Method
Mix the orange juice into the icing sugar to make a smooth batter add all the other dry ingredients with the warm melted butter. Chill in the refrigerator overnight.

## Pre-heat the oven 180°c/350°/gas 4
Pipe the mixture on to trays, lined with baking paper and bake until golden brown, cool slightly and mould into desired shape and store in an airtight container until ready to use.

# Ginger Sponge Pudding with Caramelised Apples and Caramel Sauce

## Ingredients

| | |
|---|---|
| 100g butter | 125g plain flour |
| 125g soft brown sugar | 1 teaspoon bi-carbonate of soda |
| 2 eggs | 1 teaspoon ground cinnamon |
| 1 tablespoon of black treacle | 4 pinches ground ginger |
| 125ml double cream | 1 tablespoon finely chopped |
| 1 teaspoon vanilla essence | stem ginger (optional) |

## Method – Pre-heat oven to 180°c/fan oven 160°c/ gas 4

Cream the butter and sugar until light, beat in the eggs and black treacle and fold in the cream and the vanilla essence. Sift the flour, bi-carb and spices and carefully fold into the mixture then add the stem ginger if using and mix well.

Grease 6 metal pudding moulds and place them on a baking tray, fill the moulds and bake in the oven for about 20 minutes or until they spring back to the touch.

## Apple and Caramel Sauce

280g sugar

55g unsalted butter
225ml double cream
3 peeled, cored and each apple cut into 8 segments
Pulp of a ½ vanilla bean (optional)

## Method

Put sugar into a frying pan over a medium heat and cook the sugar until it is golden brown add the apples and caramelise with the sugar until apples are golden brown, add the butter and vanilla bean pulp, cream and cook until you have a nice caramel sauce. Set the sauce aside until ready to pour over the puddings.

Warm the puddings in the oven for a few moments – set at 150°c/fan oven 130°c/gas 2

Place puddings on a plate then put the caramelised apples on top and pour over the caramel sauce. Serve with vanilla ice-cream or clotted cream.

# Apple Pancakes with a Spicy Plum Sauce

**Pancake Mix – makes About 16 Pancakes**
2 large eggs
125ml water
125 milk
110g flour
Pinch salt
2 tablespoons calvados –optional
30ml melted butter

**Method**
Put the eggs, water and milk into a stainless steel bowl, whisk them together and then add the flour and salt, stir in the butter. Add the calvados if using, refrigerate the batter for at least ½ hour to overnight. Before you use the batter strain it through a sieve.

**Buttered Apples**
175g butter
2 tablespoons brown sugar
4 eating apples, peeled and cut into chunks or quarters
1 vanilla bean, split
1 small piece of cinnamon stick or 2 verbena leafs (lemon)

**Method**
Melt the butter and sugar gently in a wide based frying pan. Add apple and spice and cover the pan tightly for five minutes until the fruit has softened. Remove lid and watch closely. Once tender increase the heat and shake gently as the apple becomes lightly caramelised. Pour out of the frying pan on to a clean tray and allow to cool.

**Spicy Plum Sauce**
500ml water
500g castor sugar
150ml cassis
100ml brandy
1 vanilla bean, scraped
½ sick of cinnamon
1kg ripe plums, halved and stoned
1 star anise

**Method**
Put all the ingredients except the plums into a large stainless steel saucepan and bring to the boil then simmer for 20 minutes. Add the plums to the syrup and cook over a low heat for 1 hour. Press the contents of the saucepan through a fine sieve. Thin down with a little orange juice if needed. Set aside.

**Assembly**
Put about 2 tablespoons of apple filling mixture on each pancake 1 inch from the edge and roll the pancake up tucking the ends in as your go. Repeat with the other pancakes and place on a baking tray, shake icing sugar on top of the pancakes and place in the oven for 5 minutes.

**To serve**
Pour the plum sauce into the middle of 4 dessert plates. Remove pancakes from the oven and place on the centre of the plum sauce and top with an ice-cream of your choice. Serve immediately.

# Chocolate Pithivier with a Tangerine Sauce

........................................................

### Ingredients
**Cream cheese dough**

225g cream cheese
225g unsalted butter
250g flour

### Method

Mix the cream cheese batter and flour until it just comes together place in a bowl and refrigerate for at least 1 hour.

### Ingredients
**Crème pâtissière**

125ml milk
½ vanilla bean, split and scraped
1½ egg yolks
35g castor sugar
2 ½ tablespoons sifted plain flour
Icing sugar for dusting

### Method

Scald the milk and vanilla bean in a saucepan over a low heat. Whisk together the egg yolks and sugar in a bowl until pale and double in volume. Whisk in the flour and continue to whisk until the mixture is smooth. Pour a third of the scalded milk onto the egg mixture and whisk thoroughly. Pour this back into the saucepan with the remaining milk, return to a low heat and cook for 5-6 minutes, stirring continuously until the crème pâtissière has thickened. Remove from the heat and pass through a fine sieve, discarding the vanilla bean. Sprinkle icing sugar on the surface of the crème pâtissière to prevent a skin from forming. Refrigerate until ready to use.

**Chocolate filling**

55g dark chocolate at least 60% cocoa solids
55g castor sugar
55g softened unsalted butter
1 egg
55g ground almonds
1 tablespoon cocoa powder
Armagnac to taste

### Method

Melt the chocolate over a bain-marie. Cream together the butter and castor sugar and stir in the egg, ground almond and cocoa powder. Add the melted chocolate and mix until the chocolate is fully incorporated. Add the Armagnac to taste. Beat the crème pâtissière into the chocolate mixture until smooth. Refrigerate for 1 hour to firm up sufficiently to roll into 60g balls. Place the chocolate balls on a tray and freeze until ready to use.

### To prepare the pastry

Roll out a third of the pastry until 2cm thick and cut out six 9cm round with a round pastry cutter. Place on a tray and refrigerate while preparing the tops. Roll out the remaining pastry 3cm thick and cut out with an 8cm cutter. Place the tops on a tray put in a fridge to rest the pastry for 30 minutes.

### Assemble the pithiviers

One at a time to prevent the pastry from becoming too warm. Place a pastry base onto a lightly floured surface. Put a chocolate ball into the centre of the pastry base and brush the edge with egg wash. Place a pastry top on the chocolate filling and mould it around the chocolate, removing any air pockets. press together well. Place the 9cm cutter over the base to cut away any excess pastry. Refrigerate while preparing the remaining pithiviers.

When all six pithiviers have been assembled, brush with egg wash and refrigerate for 30 minutes before marking.

Mark the border of the pastry at even intervals with the back of a knife. Mark the top of the pithiviers with a tip of a knife in spirals from top to bottom.

**Pre-heat the oven to 220c°/425°f/gas 7**
Bake for 8-10 minutes until crisp and golden.  **Increase the oven to 230°c/450°f/gas 8** Dust with icing sugar and return to the oven for a further 2 minutes.

**Tangerine Sauce**
3 tangerines
¼ teaspoon cornflour
30g castor sugar
A pinch of ground cinnamon
   "   "   of ground ginger
   "   "   of ground cloves

**Method**
Peel tangerines and cut into quarters, discard the pips and blend the fruit with some water in a liquidizer, strain through a sieve and divide in half.  Place one part in a bowl and dissolve the cornflour in it, put the other part in a shallow saucepan and bring to the boil with the sugar constantly stirring, add the mixture with the dissolved cornflour, bring quickly to the boil stir until you have a smooth sauce, remove from the heat and add the spices.  Keep warm.

Honey Mousse
with Port Jelly and
Fresh Raspberries

**Ingredients – Serves 6**

**Mousse**

**Sugar Syrup**

4 large eggs yolks

90ml water

100g castor sugar

80g sugar

320 ml milk

Boil until dissolved and set aside to cool,
   refrigerate when cold

60g honey

2 ½ gelatine leaves

250 ml double cream, whipped to stiff peaks

**Method**

Bring the milk to simmering point in a saucepan. Whisk the egg yolks and castor sugar in a bowl until pale and frothy, then add the honey and slowly whisk in the warm milk. Stand the bowl over a bain-marie and gently cook, whisking continuously until the mixture coats the back of a spoon.

Soften the gelatine leaves in a little cold water, wring out the excess water and stir the gelatine into the custard until dissolved. Pass the custard through a fine sieve into a clean bowl and cool over ice in the refrigerator. When the custard is almost set (about an hour) fold in the whipped cream.

**Port Jelly**

90 ml port

90 sugar syrup

2 gelatine leaves

**Method**

**To make the jelly** - Bring the port and sugar syrup up to the boil in a saucepan. Soften the gelatine leaves in a little water and wring out the excess water and stir the gelatine into the hot liquid until dissolved. Pass the jelly through a fine sieve into a bowl and allow to cool but not set.

**To assemble**

Spoon the mousse into the desired ring moulds leaving a gap at the top for the port jelly. Refrigerate until set (about 45 minutes) pour the jelly on top of the mousse. Refrigerate until set (about 1 hour).

**To serve**

Suspend the moulds in hot water for 10 seconds then carefully turn out on to shortbread biscuit in the middle of the plate. Place a few raspberries on top of the honey mousse and drizzle a little honey over the top. Delicious!!

*This is a wonderfully elegant fine dining restaurant dessert, it is simple to make and tastes divine. You can serve it with raspberry sorbet as well if you like.*

# Warm Chocolate Tart with Candied Hazelnuts

**Pate Sablé (shortbread dough)**
**Ingredients – Serves 8**
200g unsalted butter
Pinch of salt
100g icing sugar
2 egg yolks
250g plain flour
1 drop of vanilla or lemon essence

## Method

In a food processor combine the butter and salt and sugar and blitz quickly add the vanilla and eggs and blitz again then lastly add the flour. Turn the dough on to a board and wrap in cling film and chill and refrigerate for about 1 hour.

Transfer the dough to a sheet of waxed paper and with your hands gently form the dough into a ball and flatten it into a circle and then carefully roll the dough out to form a circle to fit the tin. Transfer it to the prepared tart pan. Generously prick the dough lining the bottom of the tart pan and refrigerate for at least 1 hour or up to 24 hours.

### Pre-heat the oven to 375°f / 190°c / gas 5

Remove the tart shell from the refrigerator, place on a baking sheet in the centre of the oven. Bake the pastry for 10 to 15 minutes. Cool the pastry case for at least ½ hour before filling with the chocolate mixture.

## Filling Mixture

180ml double cream
90ml milk
175g dark chocolate
1 large egg, slightly beaten

## Method
### Pre-heat oven to 190°c/375°f/gas 5

In a medium saucepan combine the cream and milk and bring to a simmer over a moderate heat. Remove the pan from the heat, pass through a sieve into a clean bowl add the chocolate and stir until the chocolate is thoroughly melted and the mixture is well blended. Set aside to cool until lukewarm. When cooled add the egg and whisk until thoroughly blended.

Pour the mixture into the prepared pastry shell. Place in the centre of the oven and bake for about 15 minutes until the filling is slightly firm but still trembling in the centre. Remove from the oven and place on a rack to cool. Serve warm at room temperature.

## Candied Hazelnuts

500g castor sugar
500ml water
1 tablespoon salt
300g hazelnuts

## Method

Boil the water, sugar and salt. Add the hazelnuts and heat to 110°c, carefully pour into a colander but do not drain or wash the nuts, place on a sheet of baking parchment and lay the nuts out flat, bake in a 180°c/fan oven 160°c/gas 4 oven until the nuts are golden brown, about 10-15 minutes. Remove and allow to cool, place in an airtight container.

# Christmas Pudding Parfait with Spiced Pecans

...........................................................

**Ingredients – Makes 1 terrine**
300g Christmas pudding
125ml brandy.

**Sabayon**
4 egg yolks
100g sugar
Juice of 1 lemon
50ml sweet wine
300ml whipped cream, beat until it reaches the ribbon stage.

**Method**
Mix all the sabayon ingredients together except the cream. Place over a bain-marie in a heat- proof bowl and beat until thick and creamy.

Remove from heat and pour into an electric mixing bowl, beat well until mixture has cooled.

Pour the brandy over the Christmas pudding and heat in the oven for 10 minutes. Remove from the oven and allow to cool for 5 minutes. Break up the Christmas pudding with a fork and with a spoon add the sabayon mixture ensuring that it is folded in well. Then fold in the whipped cream. Pour into a terrine mould lined with a freezer bag and freeze for at least 4 hours.

When frozen remove from the freezer and pour over the white chocolate glaze (see page 129), place it back in the freezer until set. Take out of the freezer and cut into the sizes you require.

**Spiced Pecans**
**Ingredients**
**Pre-heat oven 160°c/gas 3**
1 egg white
175g pecan halves
55g granulated sugar
2 teaspoons ground cinnamon
½ teaspoon freshly grated nutmeg
1 teaspoon ginger

**Method**
Whisk the egg white just until frothy, about 30 seconds. In a large bowl mix the pecan halves thoroughly with egg white. In a small bowl toss the sugar and spices together and then toss with the pecan halves, mixing well.

Spread evenly on a baking tray and bake for 30 minutes or until evenly browned. Cool.

Store in airtight jars or tins for up to 1 month.

# Rhubarb Parfait with Poached Rhubarb and Almond Cake

*This is a lovely recipe taking advantage of the early spring rhubarb*

.........................................

**Poaching Rhubarab**
12 stalks of rhubarb
100g castor sugar
30ml strained fresh lemon juice

**Method**
Wash the rhubarb and cut the stalks into 3cm lengths then cook them with castor sugar and lemon juice in a frying pan over a gentle heat until the rhubarb has softened but still holds its shape.
Remove the pan from the heat and strain the juice from the rhubarb and reserve. Allow the rhubarb to cool. Reduce the liquid slightly over heat until a little thicker.

**Rhubarb Parfait**
**Stewed Rhubarb**
500g rhubarb – peeled and cut
200g castor sugar
50ml sweet wine

**Method**
Marinate above overnight. Next day cook the rhubarb until very soft (mushy), liquidise and cool
(If too runny texture, reduce)

**Sabayon mixture**
5 egg yolks
150g castor sugar
Juice of ½ lemon
400ml double cream

**Method to make a sabayon**
Mix the egg yolks with the castor sugar; whisk the mixture in a double boiler (bain marie) over a gentle heat for about 5 minutes until the mixture is frothy and creamy and double the volume. Remove from the heat and continue to whisk until the mixture is cool, when cool fold in the rhubarb and cream. Pour into moulds and freeze.

**Soft Almond Cake**
240g ground almonds
60g self-raising flour
110g brown sugar
100g castor sugar
10 egg whites

**Method**
**Pre-heat oven 350°f/180°c/gas 4**
Mix ground almonds, flour and brown sugar. Stiffly beat egg whites with castor sugar then mix with ground almonds. Bake in a prepared cake tin for 40 minutes in the oven.

.................................................

### Chef's Tip
*Parfait is a French adjective, literally meaning 'perfect'.*
*A rich cold dessert made with cream, eggs and fruit.*

.................................................

# Passion Fruit Jelly with Rice Pudding Fritters and Indian Spice Ice-cream

. . . . . . . . . . . . . . . . . . . . . . . . . . . . . . . . . . . . . . . . . .

**Ingredients – Serves 8**
**Rice Pudding**
200g Arborio rice
450ml cream
225ml milk
Orange / Lemon zest
150g granulated sugar

In a pan bring all the ingredients up to a boil, put pudding mixture in a baking dish, cover and bake at 160c/325f/gas 3 – for 1 hour

**Passion Jelly**
100ml Orange juice
350ml Passion pulp
225ml stock syrup (see page 128)
4 leaves gelatine

**Method**
Soak the gelatine in cold water, simmer the orange juice take off the heat and add gelatine, stock syrup and passion juice, stir and pour into moulds. Set in a fridge for about three hours.

**Pastry Cream**
3 eggs yolks
75g castor sugar
250ml milk – scald
20g flour

**Method**
Beat the eggs and sugar together until creamy, add the flour and pour in the scalded milk, place into a saucepan and cook stirring constantly until the mixture thickens and the flour is cooked out.
When cooled fold pastry cream and cooled rice pudding together, pour on to a tray and cover with cling film. Allow to cool.

**Fritter Batter**
70g plain flour
70g corn flour
1 teaspoon baking powder
5g castor sugar
175ml cold water
A little ground almonds to coat the fritters

**Method**
Combine the fritter batter ingredients together

**To Cook Fritters**
**Turn fryer on to 180°c**
Quenelle the rice pudding and roll in the ground almonds and dip in the batter, place in the fryer and fry for four minutes or until golden brown. Keep warm.

**To Serve**
Turn jellies out on to the centre of the plates and drain fritters on paper and arrange around the outside of the jellies. Finish with a passion fruit pulp. I love to this recipe with Indian ice-cream; it makes an interesting and delicious combination. (See page 130).

> ## *Chef's Tip*
> *Quenelle means to shape between two spoons*

# White Chocolate Crème Brûlée with Marinated Oranges

**Ingredients – Serves 6**
225ml double cream
85ml ml milk
50g castor sugar
240g egg yolks
125g white chocolate

**Method**
**Pre-heat the oven to 275°f / 140°c / gas 1**

In a large saucepan combine the cream, milk, and sugar and bring up to a boil. Remove from the heat. In a large bowl whisk the eggs and whisk in the cream mixture quickly so that the egg does not cook. Add the white chocolate and then strain through a fine mesh sieve.

Divide the mixture among six 300ml gratin or ramekin dishes. Place the ramekin dishes in a roasting pan, slide the middle rack partially out of the oven and place the pan on the rack. Pour hot water into the pan to a depth of ¾ cup the sides of the sides of the ramekin dishes.

Very carefully slide the rack back into the oven, bake for 20 – 30 minutes or until the custard just wobbles slightly when you tap the dishes, carefully remove the gratin dishes from the water and allow to cool. Refrigerate for at least 3 hours.

**Marinated Oranges**
50g castor sugar
1 star anise
100ml water
2 tablespoons grenadine syrup
150ml strained fresh orange juice
3 oranges segmented
½ vanilla pod seeds scraped out and added to the caramel
Zest of 2 oranges

**Method**
Boil the castor sugar and water in a saucepan until the mixture turns into a caramel colour. Reduce the heat and add the orange juice and zest and cook for 5 minutes then add the grenadine syrup, vanilla pod seeds and star anise. Cook for another 5 minutes, finally pour over the segmented orange in a bowl and allow to marinate for a day.

**To Serve**
Sprinkle 1 tablespoon of sugar evenly over each crème brûlée use a hand-held blow torch (or under the grill) to evenly caramelise the sugar. Serve with marinated oranges and mint syrup (see pages 128/129).

# Spiced Pecans

**Ingredients**
**Pre-heat oven 160°c/gas 3**
1 egg white
175g pecan halves
55g granulated sugar
2 teaspoons ground cinnamon
½ teaspoon freshly grated nutmeg
1 teaspoon ginger

**Method**
Whisk the egg white just until frothy, about 30 seconds. In a large bowl mix the pecan halves thoroughly with egg white. In a small bowl toss the sugar and spices together and then toss with the pecan halves, mixing well.

Spread evenly on a baking tray and bake for 30 minutes or until evenly browned. Cool.

Store in airtight jars or tins for up to 1 month.

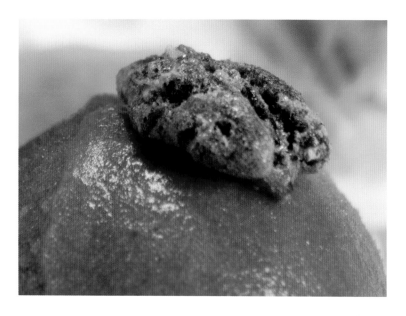

# Fruit Syrups and Sauces

**Raspberry Sauce – makes 200ml**
500g raspberries
100ml sugar syrup
25ml strained lemon juice

**Method**
Purée the raspberries, sugar syrup and lemon juice in a food processor or blender. Place in a stainless steel saucepan and reduce to 200ml. Pass the purée through a fine meshed sieve and leave to cool. Store the sauce in the refrigerator until ready to use.

**Sugar Syrup – 1.25litres**
1 litre water
1kg castor sugar

**Method**
Bring the water and castor sugar to a boil in a stainless steel saucepan. Simmer for 15 minutes, then remove from the heat and allow to cool store the syrup in the refrigerator until ready to use. It lasts almost indefinitely.

**Passion Fruit Syrup – makes 500ml**
300g castor sugar
100ml water
250ml passion fruit juice
6 passion fruits

**Method**
Bring the castor sugar and water to a boil in a stainless steel saucepan and cook without stirring over a high heat until a pale caramel colour. Add the passion fruit juice, reduce the heat to a simmer for 5 minutes then remove from the heat and stir in the pulp from the passion fruit.

Pour the syrup into a stainless steel bowl. Allow to cool and refrigerate. This syrup will keep for a few weeks.

# White Chocolate Glaze

### Ingredients
225g white chocolate
50ml double cream
1 tablespoon maple syrup
2 tablespoons lemon juice (1 lemon)

### Method
In a heatproof bowl, melt the chocolate over barely simmering water. In a saucepan, bring the cream to a simmer stir into the melted chocolate, along with the maple syrup and lemon juice until smooth.

When a spoonful of glaze is lifted it should fall in a steady stream, thin with cream if necessary, set aside.

Re-heat over simmering water to use. If the glaze is too thick it is probably not hot enough. Keep refrigerated up to one month.

# Marinated Oranges

### Ingredients
30g castor sugar
1 star anise
100ml water
2 tablespoons grenadine syrup
150ml strained fresh orange juice
3 oranges segmented
½ vanilla pod seeds scraped out
Zest of 2 oranges
and added to the caramel

### Method
Boil the castor sugar and water in a saucepan until the mixture turns into a caramel colour. Reduce the heat and add the orange juice and zest and cook for 5 minutes then add the grenadine syrup, vanilla pod seeds and star anise. Cook for another 5 minutes, finally pour over the segmented orange in a bowl and allow to marinate for a day.

# Indian Ice-cream

**Ingredients**

225ml double cream
225ml whipping cream
115g castor sugar
2 teaspoons of Darjeeling black tea leaves
½ a cinnamon stick
1 star anise
2 teaspoons fennel seeds
3 cardamom pods
3 whole cloves
½ vanilla bean, split and pulp scraped
5 large egg yolks

1 teaspoon fresh lemon juice reaches 175° on a candy thermometer or coats the back of a spoon, do not boil or the mixture will curdle. Stir in the lemon juice the cream.

**Method**

Combine the creams and ½ of the sugar in a saucepan on medium heat, bring just to the boil, stir in the tea leaves, cinnamon stick, star anise, fennel seeds, cardamom, cloves and vanilla bean pulp and pod. Remove fro the heat and cover and infuse for 1 hour.

Return infused cream to the stove which should be on a medium heat, bring back just to the boil. Remove from the heat and strain through a fine mesh sieve discarding spices. In a bowl whisk together the egg yolks and the remaining sugar until light and fluffy. Temper the egg mixtures by whisking in a small amount of the infused cream then slowly stir in the rest of the cream.

Transfer the mixture to a clean saucepan and return to the stove stirring constantly with a wooden spoon until it reaches 175° on a candy thermometer or coats the back of a spoon, **do not boil or the mixture will curdle**. Stir in the lemon juice, strain through a fine sieve and allow to cool. Place the mixture in an ice-cream maker and process according to the manufacturer's instructions.

# Lemon Curd

**Ingredients**
3 lemons - juice and zest
230g sugar
250g butter
4 whole eggs

**Method**
Mix all the above ingredients together. Whisk over a bain marie ( a large bowl sitting on a pan of water) until the mixture is thick and resembles lightly whipped cream. Set aside and leave to cool.

## Chef's Tip
*You can also turn this lemon curd mixture into a lovely light mousse for meringues by adding 300ml of lightly whipped cream or serve it with fresh fruits.*

# Tuiles Biscuits

**Ingredients**
50g unsalted butter
50g castor sugar
2 egg whites
50g plain flour

**Method Pre-heat the oven to 160°c/325°f/gas 3**
Cream the butter and castor sugar in an electric mixer until pale and creamy fold the unbeaten egg whites into the mixture a little at a time add the flour and work until the dough becomes smooth. Set aside and refrigerate.

Work the mixture while it is soft and pliable with a pallet knife; spread a thin layer of the mixture on to a non-stick mat in a desired stencil shape of your choice.

Bake the tuiles until they are golden brown, leave to cool and then place in an airtight container until ready to use.

# Sauces

# Red Wine Shallots

## Ingredients
18 shallots, peeled
400ml red wine
200g sugar
1 sprig of Rosemary or thyme

## Method
Place all ingredients in a small saucepan and simmer until the shallots are soft, about 40 minutes. Drain the shallots, retaining the cooking liquor; put the shallots into a container. Place cooking liquor back on the heat and reduce by half. Pour reduced liquor over the shallots and allow to cool.

# Beurre Blanc Sauce

## Ingredients – Serves 4
55g shallots – peeled and finely chopped
2 tablespoons white wine vinegar
3 tablespoons dry white wine
200g unsalted butter, diced
Lemon juice
Salt and freshly ground pepper

## Method
In a small saucepan combine the shallots, vinegar and wine and boil until you have about 1 tablespoon of liquid. Add 2 tablespoons of cold water then over a gentle heat whisk in the cold diced butter a little at a time until completely amalgamated. The finished sauce will be creamy and homogenous and a delicate yellow.

If you add 2 tablespoons of cream after reducing the liquid it will prevent the sauce from separating.

# White Wine Sauce

## Ingredients – Serves 4
20g x shallots – chopped
10g x butter
200ml x fish stock
½ x white part of a leek – chopped
2 x sticks of celery
150ml x dry white wine
30ml x vermouth
200ml x double cream
100g x butter – softened
Salt and freshly ground pepper

## Method
Melt 10g of butter and sweat the shallots and leeks. Add the white wine, vermouth and fish stock and reduce by two thirds. Add the double cream and reduce again. Gradually whisk in the soft butter and season with salt and freshly ground pepper.

# Sicilian Pesto

**Ingredients**
2 cloves garlic, peeled
Large handful of leaves basil
1 tablespoon of celery leaves
100 g blanched almonds, roughly chopped or pinenuts
4 sun dried tomatoes, peeled and chopped
6 tablespoon olive oil
Salt and freshly ground black pepper

**Method**
In a mortar pound the garlic and basil into a paste.
Add the almonds, little by little, pounding after each addition, then the
tomatoes. When all the ingredients are reduced to a pulp, add the
olive oil and the salt and pepper. Alternately use an electric blender, in
which case the oil should be added at the beginning.

# Chilli mango salsa

**Ingredients**
1 large mango ripe but firm
1 small red pepper, finely diced
1 small Spanish onion, medium dice
1 clove garlic
1 bird's eye chilli finely minced
Juice of 1 lime
2 teaspoons basil
2 teaspoons basil
Salt and pepper

**Mango salsa**
Cut the mango flesh into 1cm / ½ inch dice. Roast the red peppers peel
then dice and add to the mango also chopped onion, garlic, chilli, lime
juice and chopped basil. Very gently mix all the ingredients together and
add freshly grated salt and black pepper, refrigerate for at least an hour.

# Red Wine Sauce

**Ingredients**
40 ml vegetable oil
6 shallots, finely sliced
1 carrot roughly diced
1 stick of celery, diced
2 cloves garlic
2 bay leaves
10 crushed black peppercorns
2 sprigs thyme
1 sprig Rosemary
400ml red wine
200 crème de cassis
300ml chicken stock, beef stock or vegetable stock
200ml water

**Method**
Heat the oil in a large saucepan until hot, add shallots, garlic, celery
and diced carrots, cook until caramelised. Add bay leaves, peppercorns, thyme, and Rosemary. Deglaze with cassis, red wine and reduce
by two thirds. Add the chicken stock and water and reduce until the
desired consistency. Pass through a fine sieve and set aside.

Medium dice

Large dice

Concassée
(Small dice)

Brunoise

Julienne

Alumette
(matchsticks)

Rough chop

Medium chop

Fine chop

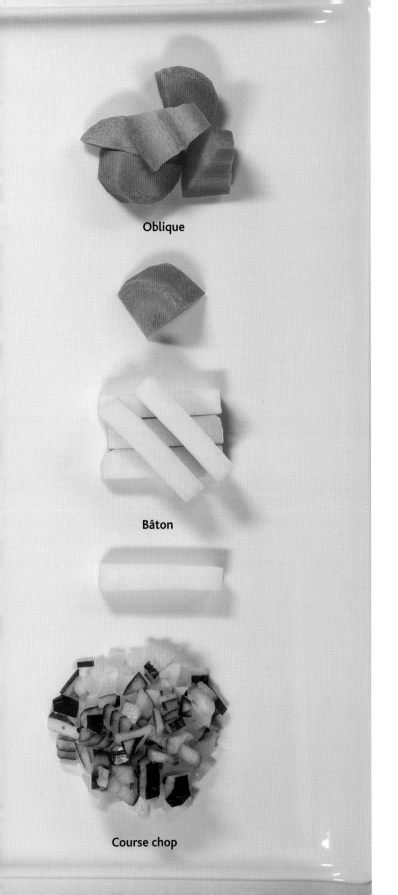

Oblique

Bâton

Course chop

# Essentials and Notes

# Italian Notes

**Extra virgin olive oil** –The results of the first cold pressing of the olives, this oil is expensive and should be used parsimoniously – literally a teaspoon at a time is sufficient. I recommend it for salads and uncooked sauces.

**Pesto Sauce** - Originated in genoa in northern Italy. Pesto is traditionally prepared in a marble mortar and ground down by a wooden pestle in a circular motion.

**Polenta** – is coarsely ground yellow or white cornmeal boiled with water, stock or milk. Polenta is originally an Italian word, derived from the word for hulled and crushed grain commonly eaten in Roman Times. It takes about 45 minutes to cook, stirring constantly. Each serving of 100g of polenta has more protein (8.1g) than one large egg. It also is gluten free

**Salsa Verde – (Green Sauce)** – 2,000 years old!! Italian salsa verde is a cold rustic sauce and includes parsley, vinegar, capers, garlic, onion, olive oil and possibly mustard.

**Prosciutto** – Made from hind leg of a pig (i.e. the ham) and outside Italy, calling it prosciutto indicates a ham that has been cured.

**Pancetta** – is cured and unsmoked this can be done simply with salt but spices and other aromatics are often added to infuse the pancetta with particular flavours.

**Ricotta** - Is an Italian whey cheese made form sheep (or cow or buffalo milk). The whey is left over from the production of cheese, ricotta literally means (re-cooked)

**Limoncello** – Is a lemon liqueur from the Amalfi coast, Calabria and Sicily. I tend to use it in sorbets and other desserts.

**Italian Flour** – Is graded by colour technically called extraction rate – that is the extent to which the bran and germ are extracted from the flour. It is marked 00 to o4 where 00 is very white and o4 is rather closer to wholemeal.

**Arborio Rice** – Is Italian short-grain rice, it is named after the town of Arborio in the Po valley, where it is grown. When cooked the rounded grains are firm and creamy and slightly chewy, thus it has a starchy taste but blends well with other flavours.

**Gnocchi** – Dumplings usually cooked in water or broth but also baked. The two principal forms are made with either potato or semolina dough. The former is used mostly in the north, the latter in Rome and the south.

# Oriental Ingredients

**Shrimp Paste (Kapi) in Thai**
A thick paste prepared from shrimps and salt, it has a very strong taste and smell. After taking kapi from the jar, smooth the remainder down well to leave the minimum surface exposed. Keep the jar well sealed or everything in the fridge or cupboard will smell of it.

**Bean Thread Noodles**
The noodles are made from green soya beans, starch and water. They come fried and look like thin brittle opaque threads. (Use in soups or spring roll fittings)

**Coconut**
This is the basic ingredient in much of south-east Asian cooking; it has no connection with the watery fluid inside a coconut. It is prepared by steeping the flesh of coconut in water. There are two types of coconut milk, thick and thin. Coconut milk does not keep long even in the fridge, freeze any you want to keep longer than two days.

**Bok-Choy**
A member of the cabbage family and is native to southern China. The leaves are mild and similar to spinach. To prepare, cut the leaves and peel the stalks, cut the stalks into thin slices cross-wise, wash well.

**Fish Sauce**
This is the basic savoury flavour of Thai cooking. Available bottled in Chinese and Oriental stores.
It is made from fermented fish or sea food.

**Rice Wine Vinegar**
White rice wine vinegar is clear and mild in flavour but has a fuller flavour than the harsh white vinegar. It is excellent in sweet and sour dishes.

**Red Rice Vinegar**
Is sweet and spicy in taste and is usually used as a dipping sauce for seafood.

**Soy Sauce is one of the world's oldest condiments.**
Soy is aged fermented soya beans, wheat and water. Japanese soy sauce is sweeter then Chinese soy.

**Sichuan Peppercorns**
Not a true pepper, these are reddish brown dry berries with a strong pungent odour, which distinguishes them from the hotter black.

**Fresh Coriander**
Other names are Cilantro and Chinese parsley.
Coriander is one of the most heavily consumed fresh herbs on our planet. Regions of use are China and South East Asia.

**Palm Sugar**
Is made by making several slits on to the stem of a palm tree and collecting the sap and the sap is then boiled until it thickens. Palm sugar should not be confused with coconut sugar which is made from the sap of the cut flower buds of the coconut palm.

# Seasonal Produce

DEVON HAS exceptional food and drink producers and I consider myself very lucky to be able to get well sourced ingredients right on my doorstep. Devon is fast becoming famous for its award winning restaurants, food festivals, markets and vineyards so eating and cooking seasonal local produce seems the obvious thing to do. Here is my guide to some of the best ingredients available and at what month of the year to source your produce, and what you should look out for on menus when dining out.

## JANUARY

Cold, rain and snow, all this and the holiday seasons has just finished. January is a dull month but I like to think of it as a culinary challenge. Turbot, native oysters, mutton, mallard, partridge, pheasant, snipe, broccoli, purple sprouting, parsnips, swede, Jerusalem artichokes, celeriac, leeks, cabbage, salsify, pennywort, forced rhubarb, quince, meddlers.

## FEBRUARY

Is the time I have to eat hearty soups and braised dishes. Rabbit, venison, pigeon, wolf fish, cuttlefish, new seasons garlic, beetroot, sea purslane, wild watercress, wild sorrel, forced rhubarb, cabbages, carrots, chicory and onions.

## MARCH

Wild salmon, scallops, elvers, Razor clams, Guinea fowl eggs, beetroot, sorrel, spinach, turnips, cauliflower, lettuce, new seasons garlic, pennywort, wild chervil, spring onions, radishes and seakale.

## APRIL

Spring finally gets into its stride and the weather starts to warm slightly. Farmers will be fertilising fields to encourage grass growth for hay and silage. December through to March you can get forced rhubarb. April is the time for outdoor rhubarb, this is more robust and flavoursome although it has not got the delicate appearance of the indoor grown rhubarb. Venison, pigeon, spring lamb, gulls and pheasant eggs, spring greens, purple sprouting, broccoli, Cornish early potatoes, Jersey potatoes, celery, watercress, morel mushrooms, spring greens, wild salmon, sea trout and herring.

## MAY

Asparagus, radishes, rocket sorrel, sea beet, sea kale, watercress, razor clams, lamb (new season) , new potatoes.

## JUNE

New season lamb, beetroot, peas, garlic, turnips, elderflower, gooseberries, mackerel, sea trout, runner beans, wild strawberries, courgette flowers, wild fennel, gooseberries.

## JULY

Salads, herbs, artichoke, globe, cucumber, blackcurrants, redcurrants, blueberries, cherries, strawberries, lobster, sand eels, samphire, rock samphire and puff ball.

## AUGUST

Is the start of the game season.  Aubergine, beans, French beans, courgettes, wild sorrel, sea purslane, peppers, loganberries, cherries, greengages, sloes, grouse, snipe, wood pigeon, sea bass, sea bream.

## SEPTEMBER

Marks a turning point in the year.  It is the end of the summer and the beginning of autumn.  September is an exciting time for chefs because we can start cooking autumnal game and still manage to harvest summer berries, while wild mushrooms  start to appear with delicious squashes and autumn berries like blackcurrants, loganberries blueberries to name but a few.

## OCTOBER

Is the month when the weather starts turning cooler and the early nights are drawing in.  I find I'm in the kitchen more experimenting with my team and working out a lot of new dishes.  Ingredients not to missed, pheasants, partridge, grouse, wild ducks, succulent squashes, native apples are in peak condition, celery, carrots, red cabbage, Jerusalem artichokes, wild sorrel, wild chervil, chanterelles, salsify and of course Brussel sprouts, hazelnuts, chestnuts and walnuts.

## NOVEMBER

Is the time for beautiful winter chanterelles they are one of my favourite mushrooms.  Black bream, herring, mussels, oysters, native bass, pike, partridge, pheasant, wild duck, teal, snipe, woodcock, parsnips, Brussel sprouts, cauliflower, red cabbage, Savoy cabbage, pumpkins, squashes, salsify, leeks, wild mushrooms, puffball, apples, Quince, pears and crab apples.

## DECEMBER

Is of course the time of the year for Turkeys, goose, hare, mallard, partridge, rabbit, snipe, turkey, woodcock, salsify, swede, watercress, chanterelles, Jerusalem artichokes, parsnips, cabbages, celeriac, celery, wood blewits, sea beet, quince, forced rhubarb, Stilton and blue Wensleydale.

# Producers & Suppliers

Gorton's kitchen prides itself in using the best seasonal and local produce available throughout the year.

The list of names is below; they are the dedicated producers and suppliers who help us to achieve this.

## Produce

| | |
|---|---|
| P&J Howells | Meat, game and sausages |
| Country Cheeses | British cheese |
| S&J Fisheries | Fish and shellfish |
| Mathew Stevens & Son | Fish and shellfish |
| Tamar View Fruiterers | Fruit and vegetables |
| Wild Hart Venison | Venison and game |
| Owens of Modbury | Coffee |
| Forest Produce Ltd | Specialist ingredients for chefs |

## Catering and Restaurant Suppliers

| | |
|---|---|
| Villeroy & Boch | Crockery |
| Robert Welch | Cutlery, utensils and chefs knives |
| Clifton Food Range | Water Baths |
| Outdoor Gourmet | BBQ and smokers |
| Jazz Power | Kitchen equipment |

**Outdoor Gourmet**
Adventures with Food Smokers, Kamados, Garden Ovens and Outdoor Cooking Equipment.
**Tel: 01364 644965**
E-mail: deancourt@outdoorgourmet.co.uk
Web: www.outdoorgourmet.co.uk

**Country Cheeses**
Gary, Elise and the team have been selling and maturing Westcountry cheeses for many years about 25 now, concentrating on the development of flavour by careful nurturing and ageing of the cheese in our own cheese cave we make the best even better. Our passion lies in all things pungently delicious. Cheese shops in Tavistock **01822 615035 Topsham and Totnes.**
www.countrycheeses.co.uk

**Owens Coffee Roasters**
Description: Owens Coffee are artisan coffee roasters, based in South Devon. We produce a range of hand-crafted Organic and Fairtrade coffees roasted in small batches with the utmost attention to detail. We insist not only on the highest quality beans, but also on their sustainability and traceability.
**New Mills Industrial Estate, Modbury, Devon PL21 0TP**
Tel: 0800 8799791  Web: www.owenscoffee.com
FB: www.facebook.com/owenscoffee
Twitter: @owenscoffee

**Robert Welch Designs Ltd**
**Lower High Street  Chipping Campden  Gloucestershire  GL55 6DY**
**UK  Telephone: +44 (0)1789 722419  Mobile: +44 (0) 7545 644325**
**Fax: +44 (0)1789 721521**
**hospitality@welch.co.uk**

**Clifton Food Range®** are British designers and manufacturers of sous vide water baths and related equipment - in use in the most acclaimed kitchens worldwide. Based in the South West of England, the family owned company are experts in temperature control technology.

(: +44 (0) 1934 626691   www.cliftonfoodrange.co.uk
Twitter: @cliftonfood

### What is The Chefs' Forum?
Throughout the year The Chefs' Forum aims to provide everyday professional needs from recruitment to produce to equipment as well as enlisting talented young apprentices from the local catering colleges and providing students with a unique opportunity to see how the industry works. The Forum provides a facility for great local chefs to share their knowledge and experience one another's kitchens. Each gathering hosts interesting and exciting speakers and demonstrations. Alongside this, quality local producers and suppliers will be invited to showcase their wares which helps support the use of their products in local restaurants. The Chefs' Forum is made up of chefs whose professional expertise has been recognised in the acquisition of prestigious foodie accreditations from Michelin Stars, AA Rosettes to Good Food Guide cooking scores.

**Tamar View Fruiterers**
Suppliers of fresh, local produce from the heart of the West Country.
Barrett House, Marjorie Court, Saltash PL12 6AY
Tel: 01752 848738
www.tamarviewfruiterers.co.uk

**Eat Out Devon,** the counties best online guide to finding great places to eat out!
www.eatoutdevon.com

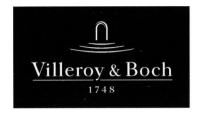

**Villeroy & Boch**
With 265 years of experience in creating sophisticated tableware, glassware and cutlery, Villeroy & Boch offers an array of designs; from country pub classic to a sleek and modern style fit for formal and contemporary dining.  For further information please call Villeroy & Boch on **0208 875 6011 or http://www.1748club.co.uk/tabletalk/**

**Adrian Oakes Photography**
Adrian is a landscape and contemporary photographer based in Exmouth, Devon where he lives with his family.  More of Adrian's work can be found at www.adrianoakes.com.